Magic for Lovers

How to use magical and astrological techniques to locate your ideal lover.

This book belongs to:
Michèle Kreft

Magic for Lovers

How to use magical and astrological techniques to locate your ideal lover

Kathleen McCormack

THE AQUARIAN PRESS

First published 1985

British Library Cataloguing in Publication Data

McCormack, Kathleen
Magic for lovers.
1. Astrology   2. Love
I. Title
133'.83067   BF1729.L6

ISBN 0-85030-468-7

*The Aquarian Press is part of the Thorsons Publishing Group,
Wellingborough, Northamptonshire, NN8 2RQ, England.*

Printed in Great Britain by Richard Clay Limited,
Bungay, Suffolk.

3 5 7 9 10 8 6 4 2

Contents

Introduction

Astrology is such an ancient science that it is difficult to pinpoint exactly where it began. We know the ancient Chaldeans practised it many thousands of years before Christ. We have discovered that the Mayans also practised it, and so did the Egyptians, the Babylonians and the ancient Greeks and Romans. But despite the spread of the Christian religion (which forbade its practice) and the rationalists and sceptics who scoffed at its theory, some early scholars still studied the heavens to ascertain our characters, our latent abilities, our moral and mental strengths and weaknesses. Through the ages, to our present materialistic time, astrology has retained its hold on the minds of men. It has fascinated some of the most formidable intellects in history, such as the astronomers Johann Kepler and Tycho Brahe, the scientist Jerome Cardan, mathematicians such as Pierre Gassendi and reformers such as Philip Melancthon. The results of their studies were tabulated and formulated as horoscopes, which were consulted avidly by the mass of the population. Today we can still see the ancient birth maps of such people as Henry VIII, William Shakespeare, Kaiser Wilhelm, Sigmund Freud and even Adolf Hitler; for the late Fuehrer kept an astrologer by him on his staff.

The characteristics of an individual born under any of the twelve signs of the Zodiac forge his destiny, influence his actions and make him the kind of person he will be from cradle to grave. As a guide to help you to understand others, astrology is invaluable — particularly if you are attracted emotionally to a person whom you've just met, but who has depths to his character which baffle and confuse you, so that you feel you will never understand him or become close.

So here are the twelve types of the Zodiac, for you to mix and match, and these in turn are divided traditionally into three Decans. So there are thirty-six individual types for you to study and compare with your friends, both male and female. There is also a chart of compatability, for you to enjoy testing, and also a section on health, so that you can learn how to cherish your lover's physical well-being when you have learned how to capture his heart. Before we go any further, there is one point that you should always remember, and that is the time of the 'cusp' birthdays.

The Cusps of the Signs

A person is born on the cusp when his birthday occurs on the very last day of one sign or until the 27th of the month. This can vary a day or so from month to month either way, but the general rule is from 20th or 21st to 27th of any month. These cusp people, because the Sun is influenced to some extent by the preceding sign for that spanning period, partake in a greater or lesser measure of the attributes of both the signs.

For instance the person born on 20 May, will have attributes of both Taurus and Gemini, while a person born on 23 July will have characteristics of both Leo and Cancer.

CHAPTER 1

Find Your Lover in the Stars

Capricorn: Male

22 December to 20 January

Ruling planet:	Saturn
Ruling symbol:	The Goat
Ruling sign:	Earth

If your lover is a Capricorn, then you will have a challenge on your hands if you wish to capture this dedicated climber. For he does not change his habits very easily and will not be made over to your specifications. Lacking in sentiment, loving affection, but unable to express it, always conscious of dignity, sexually generous, ambitious for money and position, never admitting defeat, these star types can improve with age. They always bring stability and sometimes luxury to their marriages, which are often contracted with due consideration to prestige, power and wealth.

If you are interested in a Capricorn male, you must always show him you consider him to be a person of consequence. Make no mistake about it, in his chosen field he will be! So if you are clever, and use foresight, he will be impressed by your intelligence. He will be even more impressed if you just happen to be a lot more important and better educated than any of the other females he knows.

Never judge a Capricorn's age by his looks. Because he takes the struggle for power and supremacy so seriously, he often looks older than he is when he is under forty; and can, in middle age, when he has achieved and relaxed, drop twenty years and appear misleadingly young. Never, if he is host or your escort, think him disinterested or bored. He is usually preoccupied with the details of the affair and tends to look grave when he is in reality enjoying himself immensely. He has not learned to smile enough. Good conversation attracts him, as long as there is nothing loud or undignified about it. This male does not like way-out styles of dress, so your dressing must be quiet, tasteful, preferably adorned with real pearls, cameos, or antique jewellery of quality.

Always aware of the esteem of others, he is willing to go to great lengths to preserve his good name and his public image. He is the master of social etiquette, for manners denote breeding in his eyes and foremost he is the devoted family man, revering parents, traditions, roots, and stability. He can be so careful of not upsetting the status quo, that at times one particular type of Capricorn will indulge in secret liaisons with people he considers not suitable to be taken home.

Capricorn males have a keen sense of obligation and are always conscious of repaying a favour or debt. They gravitate to professions which carry with them privilege, power, dignity and prestige. This is what they really seek, even though it may make them look as if they are obsessed with money. Even in the cases of Howard Hughes and Aristotle Onassis, the financial rewards were subordinate to the lust for power.

Their critical detachment, and ability to be able to cut out sentiment and act on facts alone, make them ideally suited to the law. Capricorns are found in the ranks of education, science, politics, economics and business administration. Their pride is enormous and in any marriage, a Capricorn male would have to be the breadwinner; but a Capricorn is capable of turning his back on marriage prospects if he weighs up the situation and decides that marriage would be an adverse step in his career, no matter how strong his feelings.

His is the sign of longevity, and it is quite possible that he will grow more charming and more wealthy year by year, provided that you give him the affection he craves, look after him well, and encourage him in his climb up the ladder. Sex is important to him for, although he outwardly favours a demure younger woman, he inwardly longs for a wife who will become a mistress when the lights are out. He is soft as butter underneath his hard shell, and only needs to be assured of your love and even more important your approval, before he will allow himself to lose his inhibitions and become more affectionate towards you.

Capricorn: Female

Capricorn females need lots of encouragement, although their facade seems self-sufficient and sophisticated. They are, in reality, a little prudish, self-contained and shy, having developed under Saturn the slow task master, and are not as sexually aware as other signs. A definite snob with regard to worldly success, manners, background and intellectuality, the Capricorn woman is an ambitious perfectionist who is more interested in the serious things of life.

Her dress is fastidiously elegant, and is always perfect for the occasion, for social etiquette to her is all important. If she plays any sport, like the male, she must excel, otherwise she would lose face in her own eyes. Her family is important, and the best way to win her, if you have passed all the preliminaries, is to woo her mother and father.

She likes to go to places that are well-known, likes to have a routine and is extremely efficient in everything she does. Her life is organized so well that any break in the smooth running of her days can throw her out of gear. She does not like to be tied or obligated to many people outside the family, except in the case of her work, into which she channels all her excess energy. She will cook well, and has a liking for health foods but does not like exotic dishes herself, and is more inclined to consider whether a thing is good for you, rather than how delicious it looks.

She has no time for people who are sorry for themselves or waste their lives, and can be quite hard and unsentimental in such cases, although her judgement is usually fair and impartial, as she, too, like the male Capricorn, does not take personalities into account when assessing a situation. This, of course, can be one of her major failings, as she lacks the imagination to feel someone else's sufferings at times and can quickly become narrow and hidebound.

Capricorn women are found as nurses, teachers, social workers, bank officials, accountants, lawyers and social reporters.

You will have no difficulty in getting your Capricorn woman to marry you once you have shown her that you depend upon her to keep your life stable and to be a helpmate while you struggle to get to the top of the tree. She will lend you money, for she is bound to have a nest egg, will run your home on oiled wheels, will do repairs and attend to taxation matters. She will even show you how fiercely the fires can burn once you have lighted that first small spark, for beneath that conservative nature there lies an adventurous Pagan longing for release.

Capricorn: First Decan

If you were born between 22 December and 1 January, you can at times be rather fickle. This is because you are indecisive and go on to something new before you have completed the project in hand.

Capricorn: Second Decan

If born between 2 and 11 January you are extremely stubborn. You are not possessed with as much energy as the rest of your signs, but you are a conscientious and steady worker. Often musicians and those allied with music are born in this decan. You are the most malleable of your sign and more likeable.

Capricorn: Third Decan

If born between 12 and 20 January, you are the leader type, through brains, determination and ambition. You invariably improve your living standards as you go through life. You are friendly and modest, but you have one failing, that of sometimes overlooking the wood for the trees.

Capricorn: Lucky Features

Lucky Colours:	Black, grey, brown and violet, dull reds and purples
Lucky Stones:	Onyx, obsidian and jet, also blood-stone, sometimes ruby
Lucky Numbers:	3 for Capricorn: 8 for Saturn
Lucky Day:	Saturday
Flowers:	Nightshade and rue
Trees:	Pine, cypress and yew
Animals:	Elephant and dog
Bird:	Owl
Metal:	Lead

Aquarius: Male

21 January to 19 February

Ruling planet: Uranus
Ruling symbol: The Waterbearer
Ruling sign: Air

The Aquarian male has as the keystone of his character, the word 'freedom'. Unlike the Sagittarian, this is not only a personal concept, but he is alike concerned with world problems and humanitarianism. Lively, rebellious and unconventional, the Aquarian is an idealistic and persuasive reformer, shunning the conventional routine of life. He is often motivated by intuitional processes which give him a keen insight into both human nature as it is today and in the future.

Because he likes puzzles of all kinds, he likes studying people, and he manages to get in a lot of people-researching while conducting his romances. When he thinks he knows all about his latest conquest, when he has her all worked out, like the solutions to a puzzle, he will move on to find another kind of human puzzle he has never encountered. Once he has the answer, the interest is gone, and he keeps looking for someone who will not bore him with her predictability.

His wry sense of humour, his candour and his self-honesty are his most appealing traits while his fine mind, his original approach to life, and his exciting personality make him a dangerously attractive but very risky marriage partner. You would meet him more easily at night, for he hates early rising and only comes alive after midday. Any profession embracing humanitarian ideals or any such movement will have more than its fair share of Aquarians. The theatre attracts Aquarians as does medicine, politics, philosophy, travel, the occult and religious vocations. To capture and retain your Aquarian male, you must always keep a little aloof, save a little of yourself so that he senses a mystery, but never let him feel he finally has found the secret part of you. Aquarians love mystery and puzzles, are always seeking the novel and exciting and grow bored and rebellious if conscious of restriction, sameness or predictability.

Although he himself is vague about time, he will always expect you to be there at home waiting for him. You will have to learn to fix all the household gadgets, cope with his weird diets, make sure he remembers to eat, and finishes the project he has on hand before starting something new, and keep him warm in winter, for he is susceptible to colds and rheumatism.

You would have to be prepared to share him with individuals and groups of people, for this sign needs human contact more than any other. His absentmindedness could drive you mad, for he could become so engrossed in mental problems that everyday considerations such as sleeping and eating would be completely ignored. Your sleep schedule would have to be changed to fit in with his late rising, late going to bed rhythm. Also you would have to be prepared to follow your Aquarian in his chosen path in life, be it contrary to everything you have been used to; knowing that it could be quite possible he could change direction in midstream, but with the confidence that whatever he did would ultimately bring satisfaction to you both, provided you guided him gently and did not apply the restraints too suddenly or too clumsily.

He himself has an inner mystery that you too must respect, for there is a core of reserve unpenetrated under his open-hearted and friendly exterior. He abhors lies and will never take a hint; instead, he will become stubborn. His dignity is offended by the slightest hint on your part of jealousy or possessiveness, he feels less of a person. Since he is always popular with the opposite sex and his manner is affectionate and friendly towards them, you could almost be excused for jealousy except that he is not by nature a philanderer, and the very tolerance, freedom and measure of trust you give him will be the chains that keep him bound to you.

Aquarius: Female

The Aquarian woman is interested in the occult and astrology and is a wonderful dancer. She dresses individually and yet at the height of fashion. Spontaneity appeals to her, not being of an organized nature, and freedom is important. She will accept you in total with no reservations, provided you can do the same with her. At times she will deliberately exaggerate and dramatize to make herself important.

Sexually, there are distinct types of Aquarian females. There is the type that makes it a minor part of her life, although she is very aware of it, and there is the other type who has no reservations whatsoever but depends on her own judgement and selective powers to prevent her from becoming promiscuous. To this female, the demand for freedom assumes paramount importance and is carried into all the other areas of her life. She is seldom shocked, very perceptive and last of all, but most important, very curious. She will want to know every facet of your character, every turn of your thoughts and all the dark secrets you have kept hidden.

This girl is not interested in your money but how you earned it. She will want to see you working, will want to know all the processes of your business and will be particularly impressed with any activity that is both practical and humanitarian. She is very generous and affectionate, not so much possessive as wanting to share or be involved in your work and life, although also quite determined to retain a certain freedom and individuality to pursue her own interests. If there can be a satisfactory balance struck, then marriage with this type could be very satisfactory. There would be nothing planned or dull, although you would find yourself longing to be alone sometimes, as you would be entertaining her diverse friends at least three times a week.

Food could be a hazard, as she might favour a vegetarian way of life, but a compromise could be arranged by learning to cook yourself.

If you are a very aggressive male then you would also have to learn to cope with your spouse's tendency to dominate in sexual matters, if she is the second of the two types. You won't have to wine and dine her in all the expensive places, nor buy her mink coats, but a dishwasher and a washing machine would be warmly welcomed by this female who loathes all kinds of housework and loves any kind of machine that will help her get through the dreary domestic chores. Once you have learned to understand her, your marriage to the Aquarian female could be exciting, rewarding, and, in later years, provided you have shared in some of her interests and vice versa, the ideal companionship.

Aquarius: First Decan
If born between 21 and 31 January you are highly intelligent and utilize all your abilities, and are a born student. Life in all its facets interests

you and nothing is too mundane or small to hold your interest. You practise more self-discipline than the other decans and your kindness is the sort that springs from the heart. Religion means a lot to you.

Aquarius: Second Decan
If born between 1 and 10 February you tend to miss opportunities because either you are dreaming of future glories or you are suspicious of people or circumstances. You tend to be stubborn and impatient and cannot take orders very easily. You are not mean, but have none of the First Decan's innate kindness, so that it does not come easily for you to love, trust or help others, but as you grow older, you mellow.

Aquarius: Third Decan
If you were born between 11 and 19 February you are intuitive and can penetrate to the heart of matters and human nature. You are highly artistic, gifted for the stage, and have enormous concentration. You do everything well, with all your heart, and cannot suffer fools or bores, because you are highly efficient and capable, and time and effort wasted is to you a crime.

Aquarius: Lucky Features
Lucky stones:	Zircon and Garnet
Lucky number:	2
Lucky colours:	Electric blue and electric green
Lucky day:	Saturday
Flowers:	Foxglove, snowdrop
Tree:	Pine
Animal:	Dog
Bird:	Cuckoo
Metal:	Platinum

Pisces: Male

20 February to 20 March

Ruling planet: Neptune
Ruling symbol: The Fishes
Ruling sign: Water

Like Gemini, Pisces have a dual nature. Their sign is two fishes swimming in opposite directions and Pisces can be both dreamy and fiery. One of the most difficult signs to understand, they seem a mixture of all the other signs plus something that makes them unique.

Sympathetic and soft-hearted, imaginative and compassionate, a Pisces can sometimes be too loving and generous for his own good. Their ultra-romantic approach, their generosity to friends whose troubles they share, their dependence on love and their attitude to money, that of utilization not accumulation, leaves them particularly vulnerable to someone who is unimaginative, critical, unloving and money hungry. These people are possessed of psychic gifts enabling them to penetrate occult mysteries, yet they can be the biggest self-deceivers in the Zodiac. They never like to look directly at you, preferring to slide their eyes away, nor will they make a decision or give a direct answer unless forced to. Intent on keeping his innermost secrets hidden even from himself, the Pisces male tends to drift along in life, loving and giving, absorbing influences from those he is closest to, enjoying his food, his artistic profession or outlet and making an art of romantic love.

Criticism will kill him, but suggestion will activate him into doing those things you know have to be done. He will sympathize with your moods, divine your wants instinctively, is a sucker for stray animals and lame ducks and is sensitive to atmosphere like a plant to the sun. He will be found anywhere among the arts, in the theatre, the advertizing world, the beauty business, pure research fields, and, surprisingly enough, in any field that looks after large sums of invested capital such as banks and investment corporations.

Wear subtle shades for this man, no overbold prints or harsh colours; accentuate the feminine with flowing hair, and delicate perfume. Treat him gently, woo him slowly — do not rush him. Don't try to jump into the conversation when you feel it lagging, let it meander along, with comfortable silences and feel him relax. Don't raise your voice, keep it soft, and if your furnishings are subdued, your lights low and you have cooked a delicious meal for him, you may succeed in keeping him by your side. He is fascinated by occult matters, has a lively mind and wide assortment of friends, some of whom he has been helping over stiles for years. He is oddly secretive, living with an unworldly attitude towards material success, but if you are loved by a Pisces man, you have tasted the nectar of the gods!

Pisces: Female

The Pisces woman is even more vulnerable than her male counterpart. She has her own picture of what love should be and if you do not live up to that picture, she will feel betrayed and bereft, and could become bitter or unbalanced. Always looking for someone to live for, someone to belong to, someone to revolve around, this girl is trusting, romantic, delicate and absolutely feminine. Efficient but erratic, she will never seem to be on top of the housework because she lacks the ability to organize her practical life, and yet unless she has some creative outlet, such as writing or painting, her inner life of phantasy and imagination will in times of stress lead her into melancholia and moods of deep depression. Often a health food faddist, she can also be a heavy smoker. She likes late nights and hates early mornings; and frequently tries to attempt too much physically, which makes her irritable and tired.

Found in the theatre and the ballet, or a profession connected with the fine arts, she is inclined to romanticize events and can shut her mind to what she does not want to see, so that sometimes, if she wants to initiate a particular course of action, she is able to act immorally because of her ability to deceive herself. She is sympathetic and intuitive, making a fine helpmate for the right man who will relish her attention and devotion, shrug off her possessiveness and understand her, so that her vulnerability will be protected.

Pisces: First Decan
If you were born between 20 February and 1 March, although you

are ambitious and crave recognition and appreciation, you hold yourself back by too much caution at times. You love entertaining people, and are often drawn to catering and hotel management.

Pisces: Second Decan
If born between 2 and 10 March you could sometimes live in a sea of troubles, on your own little island unaware the world is only a handclasp away from your door. Because of your predilection to bring domestic upheaval around yourself, through over-emotionalism and unrealistic attitudes, you can achieve little in life until over forty.

Pisces: Third Decan
If born between 11 and 20 March, you are too impractical at times, but have great self-confidence, and can analyse a problem and get to the heart of the matter through logic. You are restless and love travel, particularly on the water. Your profession in life should be something that serves humanity, for you are a giver and wish to contribute more than the other two decans.

Pisces: Lucky Features
Lucky colours:	Purple, mauve and sea green
Lucky stones:	Sapphire and emerald
Lucky numbers:	6 for Pisces; 3 for both Jupiter and Neptune
Lucky day:	Thursday
Flowers:	Heliotrope and carnation
Trees:	Willow and elm
Animals:	Sheep and ox
Birds:	Swan and stork
Metal:	Tin

Aries: Male

21 March to 21 April

Ruling planet: Mars
Ruling symbol: The Ram
Ruling sign: Fire

Challenge and variety are the cornerstones of this sign. To win this natural leader you would have to let him do the chasing, and give him a balance of submission and independence. For a clinging brainless female would bore Aries sick. There is no fun without fire to an Aries, so he wants an equal; a high-spirited intelligent adversary in the struggle for domination. There will be little peace, but lots of excitement, sex, passion and interesting experiences.

However, the Aries man can be white hot one moment and finished with the whole thing the next. He is unpredictable, has an enormous ego and sex drive, unlimited amibition, the lover of power and the desire to be at the centre of the stage. Crossed in love, they can rival the Scorpio for vindictiveness, and their ego demands *they* walk away from *you*, not the other way around. Vibrant colour turns them on, so no pastels for this man. He admires high fashion, something that singles you out of the crowd so that his friends envy him and admire you.

Innovators and explorers, Arians hate to be burdened with possessions, like to live and dress casually, have no great love for food except as a replenishment for energy, and love dangerous sports, such as speed racing, the space race, and anything pertaining to fighting and war. They make excellent entertainers of every kind, as, like Leo, they are at home with the public and love to be the centre of attention.

They often gravitate to businesses that cater to the public entertainment such as bistros and bars, to which they can bring their own individual stamp or atmosphere and which gives full play to their exuberance and love of an audience.

To an Arian life is a series of conquests and all the world is his rival. He often makes alliances or is attracted to women who are already attached or tied in some way. They seem to appeal to his predatory instincts, his desire to triumph over his adversaries, for Aries is a pirate at heart, and life is a succession of challenges, struggles and prizes to be won.

To attract an Arian, although his intensity can leave you breathless, you must never appear to be interested, but remain aloof, independent, and, above all, a little challenging. Not for him the faithful sweetheart, pining her heart out. He prefers the adaptable, variable personality with a strength and fire that challenges his masculinity. He is a romantic where women are concerned, so keep such personal details as hair rinses or eyelash curlers strictly to yourself.

You must share his views, and agree with nine tenths of them or you are against him and being disloyal. He himself can agree to disagree with your views, and can in time become very dogmatic and opinionated if not gently teased out of this attitude. He will try to dominate your personality from the moment you meet to your dying day, but if you wish to hold your Arian, never allow him to feel he has the whiphand. It is then you will lose him completely and he will seek someone else who offers a new challenge. Arians never realize what they themselves often do to their lifemate, and many complain in the divorce courts, often after lengthy marriages, that their wife is no longer the woman they married and that there is nothing left of the original relationship.

Aries: Females

Often blessed with a masculine approach and a logical, direct type of mind, these natives find themselves working in fields that are traditionally male. Often she can be found in law, in journalism, in medicine, in architecture, the police force and sometimes in the dangerous speed sports such as car racing and flying. The little theatres where acting is a hobby abound in Arian talent as well as the professional theatres. Many make fine directors.

Travelling appeals to the Arian female. She likes her man to look elegant, with quiet conservative clothes of the finest quality, impeccable manners and an immaculate appearance. Although her self-reliance and independence sometimes make nonsense of the little masculine courtesies, she has a strong vein of sentimentality which makes her prefer small gifts and sincere words to ostentatious displays, which embarrass her. She does not like to be rushed, as she is suspicious of anyone who might deprive her of her freedom or put limitations on her in any way.

She is not a home body, although she is super-efficient in the home, organized beforehand, geared to saving time and efficient methods of work, and a good plain cook. She is a career woman with a built-in complex of indispensable ability. In love she is direct and masculine in her approach, and will not hesitate to take the initiative if she thinks it is necessary. Her faults are lack of tact and a certain lack of subtlety or mystery. The love of the chase often makes Aries women seem shallow and grasping, as they triumph frequently over their less endowed sisters by displaying their conquests and then losing interest.

She is strong, secretly wanting to be mastered and despising the weak. The challenge of a strong uninterested male is enough sometimes to set her hunting. She has an enormous ego and belief in her attractions and many times, through the sheer force of this self-belief, she can convince others that she is something extra special. She is a loyal partner, acknowledging no fault, but expects you to share her every sorrow and joy. Like the male, though, her failing is that she wishes to possess you utterly but not be possessed herself, while her built-in suspicion makes her a prey to jealousy, which has led to many broken romances.

Frequently she will sponsor causes, and do much charity committee work, usually as Madame President. This is more common in cases of frustration in marriage. Her failing here is that although her energy and dynamism are an inspiration to all, her intolerance and rigidity, her belief that she is the only one entitled to have opinions will often undo all the valuable work she has done.

Aries: First Decan
If born between 21 March and 31 March you tend to be very impulsive and have a very explosive temper. You are also imbued with the ideal of service to the community, and could enter politics.

Aries: Second Decan
If born between 1 April and 10 April you are affectionate and steady, honourable and faithful. You may appear placid and malleable, but you will always get your own way in the end, with the minimum of friction.

Aries: Third Decan

If born between 11 April and 21 April, you are the most typically Arian of the three. You alternate between highs and lows, are impetuous and loving, and will fight to the death for a friend or loved one. The two sides of your nature are apparent in this decan. You can be cocksure and vain, yet sensitive, jealous and unsure of yourself. Most Arians are protective of weaker people they like, and often touchingly grateful for kindness and favours shown to them.

Aries: Lucky Features

Lucky colours:	Bright yellow, bright green and bright pink, red, white
Lucky numbers:	7 for Aries, 9 for Mars
Lucky stones:	Ruby, bloodstone, diamond
Lucky day:	Tuesday
Flowers:	Gorse, wild rose and thistle
Trees:	Holly, hawthorn and chestnut
Animals:	Tiger, leopard, ram
Bird:	Magpie
Metal:	Iron

Taurus: Male

22 April to 21 May

Ruling planet:	Venus
Ruling symbol:	The Bull
Ruling sign:	Earth

Practicality, honesty, simplicity and conservatism sum up the chief characteristics of the Taurean male. He is stubborn and persistent both in his wooing and in the general concerns of life. Basically loyal, he also hates to admit he has made a mistaken choice, so that Taureans often hang on in associations that are unfortunate, injurious and even destructive. The only sign that can salvage friendship from a fiery affair, Taureans can be great haters when finally aroused, but basically lazy and well-meaning, it takes a lot to rouse their ire. However, when really angry, he will show so little restraint that he can damage himself or his own concerns in his desire to wreck vengeance. Slow to make attachments and judgements, once he has made up his mind, you will never change it, nor will he be influenced in any way.

Sexy in a basic, honest and natural way, the Taurean has great magnetism and charm. His passion and downfall can be food, but also he is sometimes inclined to take all appetites to the extreme. Sensory and down to earth pleasures are his. He is possessive, and rates his marriage partner as his most prized possession, and this may be in competition with priceless art treasures and antiques, for Taureans love to collect art for art's sake, and also because they love to preserve the traditional and historic.

He is not a lover of active sports though many are passionately attached to their gardens, and some are attracted by the game of golf because of its relatively placid pace and surroundings. They love the countryside and trees and are always happier when they have a little land or farm of their own tucked away as an investment.

They are attracted to a soft, feminine woman who would make a wonderful mother, and particularly one with a beautiful face and expressive hands. Ruled by Venus, they are particularly attracted by beauty in any shape or form, and are susceptible to surroundings to such a degree that a colourless drab atmosphere will make them moody and depressed. They value the more solid things in life, and can be over-materialistic and security-ridden; however, they are also the most wonderful providers and devoted husbands of the Zodiac, and the most capable, apart from Cancer, of enduring the monotonous period of boredom in marriage.

You will find them in all places connected with food, also real estate and farming, market gardening and landscape gardening, the building trades, vineyards, grocery businesses and in the theatre, particularly the musical side. Many famous singers are born under this sign, for it rules the throat, and most of these have a permanent battle with weight control, for all Taurean natives love their food, particularly the sweet things.

Taurus: Female

Usually physically attractive with a lithe, sexy walk, with soft rounded contours and big expressive eyes, she carries an aura of motherliness and placidity under which is barely concealed a basic sensuality. It has nothing to do with the coquette but is as natural to her as breathing, and is accepted by her as being part and parcel of her personality so that she does not use her sex consciously as a weapon. In fact, there is a great deal of the element of giving comfort in this sexuality and a basic honesty in approach. She seeks security, both emotional and economic, idealizes beauty, respects success, wants dependability and lives for the day when she can look after you.

Quality is her watchword, in everything. If you are the lucky man then you can look forward to luxurious surroundings, or at least extremely durable comfort, wonderful meals, flowers everywhere, a well-ordered routine that only an earthquake could alter, and healthy and well-mannered offspring to look up to you as the ultimate authority. Not for this woman the desire to dominate. She is won by deeds not words, and once she is yours, you have her whole undivided love and attention.

Colour means a lot to her; flowers, little animals, anything pertaining to nature, particularly perfumes, for she is a sensuous woman easily roused in lovemaking to a warm and passionate response. She loves the opulence and texture of velvets and furs, is attracted like Capricorn to the outward trappings of success, but has a surer instinct, even a psychic or intuitive sense which makes her a keen judge of people, so that outward appearances will never really fool her, for she is no snob. As a wife this woman will never fail you, and your life will be secure and rooted in the things that have enduring values.

Taurus: First Decan

If born between 22 April and 30 April the stubborn and lazy elements in your character are often predominant. You will like food very much and can be argumentative and more fiery than the next two decans.

Taurus: Second Decan

If born between 1 May and 10 May you have both discrimination and vast selectivity and control. This would make you an excellent stock-broker, buyer, fashion editor, and co-ordinator. Your tendency to hoard, not merely to save, could make your thriftiness seem meanness, and in some cases, make it hard for you to part with anything that you have had for some time.

Taurus: Third Decan

If born between 11 May and 21 May, you have an essential refinement that somehow prohibits swearing overduly, and smutty, bawdy emphasis on sex. You are reliable and stable and extremely generous and a thoroughly nice person.

Taurus: Lucky Features

Lucky colours	Blue, indigo, purple
Lucky stones:	Sapphire, emerald, turquoise, ruby and moss agate
Lucky numbers:	6 for Taurus and Venus
Lucky day:	Friday
Flowers:	Violet, rose, myrtle, lily-of-the-valley
Trees:	Sycamore, walnut, ash, apple and almond
Animal:	Bull
Bird:	Dove
Metal:	Copper

Gemini: Male

22 May to 21 June

Ruling planet:	Mercury
Ruling symbol:	The Twins
Ruling sign:	Air

Geminis are baffling, elusive, mercurial, curious, aware, restless, versatile and always on the go. A better marriage risk as they reach the thirties, for they are at heart children who do not want to grow up. A Gemini man has a quick grasp of essentials and a wonderful vocabulary, giving him the outward attributes of a highly learned pedagogue, but because of his curiosity and love of variety, his learning can be superficial, and his arguments glib and facile.

He is attracted by a witty, intelligent woman far more than by a sultry sex symbol, but cannot be bothered with a lengthy wooing.

There is too much to see and do, and too little time to do it in. Be prepared for the fact that he loves variety, and when young, is not so much promiscuous as restless, always seeking for the novel and unexplored, and enjoy your whirlwind romance even if he won't stop talking in bed. He usually is happiest when doing two jobs, running two romances or doing two things at the same time. He changes direction even in career, so that he often ends up as jack of all trades, master of none, and loves to travel because that way he does not become bored, and boredom is like a little death to him.

He is the super salesman, has a flair for improvization and a biting wit. He could be one of a set of twins, incidentally, but will have no abiding passion for the old home town. Big cities fascinate him, and he can be found in the theatre, politics, photography classes or art classes, where he may well be the teacher — for he does have a gift of imparting knowledge — or playing musical instruments; the ability to combine manual skill with mental dexterity is one of the characteristics of the Gemini subject. Lawyers, particularly barristers, disc jockeys, demonstrators, all have a large percentage of Gemini subjects in their ranks.

To win a Gemini you must move at his fast pace. Don't consider his wishes too much, but be independent in your leisure time. Learn to go along with whatever the current craze is and get used to his unpredictability. Don't let him think you missed him when he doesn't call, or just drops out of your life for a month while he takes a trip on the spur of the moment to go skiing.

Be a quick-change artist with your clothes and hairstyle so that you can confuse him as to what kind or type of a girl you are, for Gemini men love to be able to type everything. Find new things to interest him, feed him all the gossip (he loves it), the new jokes, and make lots of sparkling conversation over dinner.

Dinner itself could be a problem, for he hates organized over-formal meals, but invite all your most charming friends, women, too, and let him have verbal indigestion. He will never rove unless you allow him to be bored or feel unappreciated, for this man is a child, a charming child, with all the demands of childhood inherent in the relationship. He is impatient, particularly with illness, but woe betide you if he becomes ill himself; then you will have to play a devoted Florence Nightingale twenty-four hours a day. Exciting, exasperating, inconsistent, yet warming and companionable, the Gemini man is hard to forget once you have him in your system.

Gemini: Female

Impulsive, variable, curious, adaptable, idealistic, the Gemini girl is a mass of contradictions, of up and down moods and inconsistencies which make her a fascinating partner. Writing ability comes easily to all Gemini subjects, but the female Geminis also gravitate to public relations, promotions work and the teaching profession. Outwardly fun-loving, she has a serious side that longs for security and balance. She, like her male counterpart, can be in love with two people at the same time, loving them for different qualities. But if forced into a choice, she would either walk away from both, or pick the more secure type, provided he has as fine a sense of humour as she has herself, for this is the one thing a Geminian appreciates above all else.

Unpredictable in her movements, it is no use tying a Gemini down to any kind of schedule. She needs a safety valve or some kind of diversion or she will blow up. She must keep a little of her own world private or she will feel that killing sense of restriction and possession which can almost cause her to have a breakdown in health. She loves surprises, eating out where there are bright lights and people, going to the theatre, doing crazy things on the spur of the moment, reading on rainy days, going on long cruises, dancing till dawn, and does not require a lot of money to make her content. The sense of security and balance must be there in her partner, but the lack of actual cash does not worry her, as she can be pleased by so little and interested in anything new or strange. She is very vulnerable in that she cannot quite see her faults or failings as others can, yet knows she needs a strong steadying hand to keep her content and faithful; yet the rein must appear to be loose, and the man must be very understanding.

Often a poor sleeper, she needs to have regular meals as well as regular hours to keep her health good, and something which occupies both her hands and her mind to keep her occupied and happy. If you can meet her every mood and match her every side, then you will have a loving, exciting and charming mate.

Gemini: First Decan

If born between 22 May and 31 May you are a true Gemini in most respects. Your love of variety and change make it difficult for you to settle to anything or achieve much while you are young. As you grow older some interests predominate, and you will follow one of these to limited success.

Gemini: Second Decan

If born between 1 June and 10 June your personality is better balanced than those of the First Decan. Your faculty for criticizing and analysing can be used profitably, in pure research or teaching, writing or speaking. You will achieve success and advancement.

Gemini: Third Decan

If born between 11 June and 21 June, you are really the most sensitive of this sign and are nice to know. Your heart goes out to people, you love children and animals and you are kind, loyal and gregarious. You hide your vulnerability under an insouciance that can make you seem frivolous and empty. Your only danger is of being influenced overduly by others and led into extremes of conduct through your desire to be popular.

Gemini: Lucky Features

Lucky colours:	Silver, yellow, bright green and white, orange, yellow
Lucky stones:	Agate, chrysophras, diamond, jade
Lucky number:	5
Lucky days:	Sunday and Thursday
Flower:	Snapdragon
Tree:	Elder
Animals:	Dog or squirrel
Birds:	Parrot, linnet
Metal:	Quicksilver

Cancer: Male

22 June to 23 July

Ruling planet: The Moon
Ruling symbol: The Crab
Ruling sign: Water

The children of the Moon, Cancer subjects seem to be influenced by the Moon to a greater degree than any other sign. As the tides ebb and flow with the influences of the Moon, so do Cancer's moods swing like a pendulum. Their love life is also affected by the phases of the Moon. This vacillation is only on the surface. For Cancers are steady, sometimes bound by tradition, dependable, hearth-and-home lovers, creative but not avant-garde, sensitive, shy and easily hurt.

The crablike shell these native hide under never allows you to see too deeply into the sensitive depths. The side-like motion of the crab's gait is akin to the way Cancer subjects sometimes side-step important or unpleasant situations or decisions. They are, like the crab, tenacious, and when in love are determined and constant. The male, however, is often a one-woman man, who will not be interested in any save his ideal woman, although his charm is immense and his appeal for women very strong. Often they marry late in life, because of a sense of perfection and cautious streak that prevents them from putting themselves into a position where they could become terribly hurt, for marriage and the home are a sacred trust to them, and they want happiness that will last.

Atmosphere is very important to a Cancerian, he drinks it in, and is more interested in getting the whole overall picture than little details. His home will be a work of art, for he would be miserable living in an atmosphere that wasn't restful as well as beautiful.

Cancer subjects are strongly psychic, giving them an intuitive knowledge and an awareness of others. People confide in Cancer, but he is very secretive about himself. He is a charming host and excels on his own home ground, loves cooking and food, and all things traditional pertaining to furniture and possessions. He is a hoarder of the past. His memory is long and accurate. His taste is for the quality things — gimcrack ornaments and plastic things are not for this man. He is careful with money but not mean because he demands the best, so that he will save to obtain it. Atmosphere is to him of supreme importance, and because he is often a little shy, an extroverted, warm loving girl will often attract him like a magnet.

He loves parties and sports centred around the sea, but he is also devoted to spectator sports, and a regular football fan. He can also make a clever writer, but the subject must be something he is interested in, otherwise he loses interest very quickly. He will make a devoted and faithful husband as long as he is appreciated and loved, all the time, for his sensitive nature makes him vulnerable to coldness, sarcasm and quarrels — so much so that he can become physically ill through any sustained discord. This can cause nervous asthma and nervous disability. He has tenacity and determination and with the right partner can achieve the heights.

Cancer: Female

Cancer women go through stages, and although they commence their adolescence as dreamy eyed and idealistic, their practical home-making sides take over as they grow older and they become more money-conscious. They, like the males, demand the best quality in everything and this means men, too. Used to male attention, and this in part because of their deceptively fragile air, they are usually past masters at adornment and present a very glamorous feminine appearance with a softness about them that never leaves them. Feelings of insecurity and doubt at times make her vulnerable to criticism and rejection, and she will crave compliments and reassurance. A solid practicality, a hoarding of household goods, a healthy bank deposit and a good knowledge of cooking also go with this Cancer girl who can cry at an old movie, dress with such imagination she seems to have a film star wardrobe, and sometimes be so dreamy and absent-minded you could shake her.

Anything she does must have touches of beauty about it. Your courtship must be the conventional kind, where you, the big strong male, come to sweep her away. Not for this girl the come-hither looks and the little signs to help you along the way. She is psychic to a very great degree, so she knows the way you are feeling, but she will insist on playing the little helpless female to your big strong male, because this is the traditional romantic way. All your married life she will make you feel you are the big strong breadwinner, even though you know that underneath she has a strength and spirituality that will endure hardships with you without complaint. She will love you if you remember anniversaries (even of the day you met) birthdays, and especially if you take her out to celebrate often. Allow her to give parties for her friends and don't quibble when the bills come in for new dresses or beauty treatments. Keeping herself beautiful is a solemn duty to this girl; in the same way she beautifies her home and every meal she serves. She will mother you as well as the children, and then within hours be curled up in your lap while you fuss and comfort and baby her, secure in the knowledge that the balance of your relationship will never be impaired by outside agencies while you can keep this pendulum, of give and take, advance and retreat, the dreamy and the practical, swinging for both of you.

Cancer: First Decan
If born between 22 June and 1 July you are persistent in furthering your progress in life, you are gentle and overly sensitive, prone to jealousy and fits of depression and self-doubt. You should always live close to the sea, for the sea can soothe and comfort you.

Cancer: Second Decan
If born between 2 and 12 July, you are among the strongest people of this sign. Usually possessing charm and poise, with strong physique and good looks, you have a tenacity and appetite for life that sweeps all before it. It is difficult to refuse you anything, if you put the charm on. Your nature is not so nice if upset, for you can be malicious and envious of others, go out of your way to make trouble, particularly if jealous, and never forget an injury no matter how slight.

Cancer: Third Decan
If born between 13 and 23 July you are among the most pleasant of the Cancer group and would be a good friend to have around at all times. You are gentle, sympathetic, kind-hearted, patient and forgiving. You do not seem to achieve success when young, but usually start

your middle age in increasing comfort.

Cancer: Lucky Features

Lucky colours:	Emerald, green, white
Lucky stones:	Pearls and moonstones
Lucky numbers:	2 for Cancer and 7 for the Moon
Lucky day:	Saturday
Flowers:	Poppy, water-lily
Trees:	Willow, sycamore
Animals:	Otter and seal
Birds:	Seagull, owl
Metal:	Silver

Leo: Male

24 July to 23 August

Ruling planet:	The Sun
Ruling symbol:	The Lion
Ruling sign:	Fire

Leo men, wherever you find them, are, and must always be, the centre of the stage, both in love and in life, for they will brook no rivals. Often the sign of stage personalities, a Leo's exuberance, his pride, his stunning warmth of personality and his gregariousness make him an ideal subject for this medium. Leo men want to rule, yes, but they hate an easy conquest. Challenge is the spice of life to them, and a little bit of struggle doesn't do a Leo any harm. He is the royal sign of the Zodiac. With it go all the marvellous attributes like honour, pride, warmth, love, enthusiasm, passion, tenderness, and conversely, the other side offers arrogance, conceit, domineerance, love of luxury, and a destructive jealousy. He delights in entertaining, loves the high spots, but often doesn't worry where his next pound note is coming from.

He is impressed by surroundings (Leos can be snobs), he's lucky (because of his positive optimism, it is said), he's loyal, if you are a friend, he is a wonderful lover, a fine athlete when young, retains this vigour longer than most other signs, and knows how to dress the stage of life so that every entrance he makes is that of a star. He is finely attuned in the matters of the heart so that he can vary his approaches, from tender and quiet to passionate and tempestuous; never underhand, never boring, never in danger of losing control of the situation. His jealousy is the only big snag, for he will brook no rival, and needs constant love and affectionate reassurance to make him feel secure with you. Otherwise he will give way to jealous rages. He will always need to know he is boss, and will tend to sulk if matters go against him. The only remedy for this or for any other crisis in your relationship is to flatter him and then flatter some more. He wants to be admired all the time (his vanity demands it), and particularly if you or someone has injured his pride, flattery is the only remedy.

Leo men will often be in the public eye. If they are in an office or indoor work they are usually in an executive position, and often are found in the legal profession, and the armed forces, as well as advertising and the theatre. You will always have to provide an audience for your Leo mate, and be content to be bossed around and managed. However, he will be proud to take you out, even to go shopping with you (he has excellent taste) and will give you a lifetime of love and devotion provided you are careful never to hurt his dignity, to apply the flattery when needed, and to reassure him constantly with attention and affection.

Leo: female

The Leo lady is not quite as basic and simple as the Leo male. She is inclined to be a snob, only because she demands the best and knows where she should be. If you can't put her there, then bow out of the race. She has a very solid appreciation of money and will often pursue a very highly paid career after marriage. Her energy is such that if she becomes bored she could become destructive either with herself or with others, so for her own sake, she feels it is better to develop her talents.

Clothes are all important to this female, they must be the best and be in the height of fashion. She loves to meet people, but usually people who have made some mark in the world. Her household furnishings will be the very best, her dinners will be perfection, with every detail planned, she will feel qualified at times to give you advice on business matters, and usually her views will be sound and helpful. She will manage you as well as the children, dazzle your friends with her personality, and her sexual energy never diminishes.

However, her Leo jealousy is present, and can result in your friends being vetted and your activites being curtailed, if she becomes suspicious. Because the ever-present need of reassurance and affection is even greater in the Leo female, the results of suspicion will make her unsure, and you will have to give her large dollops of appreciation and even larger dollops of flattery. For such an intelligent woman, this is her Achilles heel, for through her vanity she can often get her judgement way out of proportion, and this type of woman can become domineering, egocentric and hard to live with. Yet, if the Leo woman is treated with love and respect she makes one of the most satisfying partners of the entire Zodiac. Her frankness, her Rabelaisian sense of humour, her magnificent sexual ardour, her homemaking and her love of gaiety and the good life all combine with her affectionate and warm personality to make the right man a wonderful companion throughout a life that will be full of enthusiasm and excitement.

Leo: First Decan

If born between 24 July and 1 August you are a faithful honourable person who loves to mix with people, go to parties and learn all the latest songs and scandals. Your only failing, if a female, is the love of personal adornment which can be excessive, leading you into extravagance and the consequent vanity which could alienate your friends.

Leo: Second Decan

If born between 2 and 12 August, you are extremely ambitious and have loads of confidence. Your bent should be law, as you can marshal facts and see flaws very quickly. Your faults, if carried to extremes, would be your penchant for bossing others, and your outspokenness.

Leo: Third Decan

If born between 13 and 23 August these are the impulsive, impatient people who sometimes give up striving when things become difficult because they can't be bothered trying any more. They are affectionate, generous and kind, and need someone behind them to keep their noses to the grindstone.

Leo: Lucky Features

Lucky colours:	Gold, orange, yellow, light green and white
Lucky stones:	Amber, topaz, tourmaline, sardonyx, ruby
Lucky numbers:	4 for Leo; 1 for the Sun
Lucky day:	Sunday
Flowers:	Marigold, sunflower, cowslip, heliotrope
Trees:	Palm and laurel
Animal:	Lion
Birds:	Cock, eagle
Metal:	Gold

Virgo: Male

24 August to 23 September

Ruling planet:	Mercury
Ruling symbol:	The Virgin
Ruling sign:	Earth

A sign that is almost contradictory, Virgos are the hardest of all the signs to get to know. Clean, neat, meticulous in habits, almost with a connotation of purity, the Virgo man is an enigma, sometimes to himself. There seem to be two types. One type will indulge in lots of short, meaningless affairs that touch him only lightly; the other type will develop a relationship first from friendship through to romance and will, if the partner is suitable, marry her after a long gradual courtship. They seem to be 'the cats who walk by themselves' and intrigue other signs, for they show a surface warmth and sparkle yet clearly, underneath, they are alone and aloof. They are quite self-sufficient, as they appear to be, which is a little frightening to most people. Their manner is always self-assured, and they carry their own very tangible dignity with them.

Their appearance belies them in many ways, their smiles and their eyes are usually warm and beautiful, they seem to be ageless, and are often found in the charitable and humanitarian organizations which cater to people's needs. Their need seems to be service to others, and many of their activities even in their spare time will be found to encompass their principles. However, they are too analytical and over-critical at times to be able to make and hold friends. They must learn to put constructive suggestions after they have exposed the weaknesses in other people's lives and plans.

Virgos seem to cling to their own immediate friends and do not make new friends as easily as most of the other signs. They have a tendency to live in the past a little, and to cling to things from the past when it is time to discard them. Work to a Virgo is as important as his friends, for it is often work that has social value. Although many financiers and millionaires are born under Virgo, money as such or even power and authority do not seem to turn this sign on.

Teachers, nurses, historians, librarians, tax consultants, accountants, musicians, and anything pertaining to the critical faculty such as music critics, mathematicians, scientists are many of the professions in which you find Virgos. To interest this stellar type you would require a lot of patience, and also a lot of ingenuity. Perhaps you could ask his help with a problem you have encountered either in your neighbourhood or at work which involves people, for your Virgo is very interested in people, as long as they keep their distance. Make sure your flat is scrupulously tidy, and that everything is in the correct place, and that includes your clothes and make-up. If you are content to build up to intimacy by a series of evenings where you discuss the political situation or the latest best-seller, you may have a good chance of snaring your Virgo male, particularly if you, yourself, are in a profession allied to his and available when he is feeling like a little companionship.

Virgo: Female

Usually beautifully groomed, with discreet make-up, this girl will have a mind and opinions all her own. She is a fanatic regarding details and will not relish being kept waiting more than one second for her first date, which could be your last if you have not attended to all the arrangements so that it goes smoothly. She is not demonstrative and does not enjoy petting or kissing, and if she allows you to hold her hands in the car, then you can take it that you have made second or third base.

She appreciates art in its highest form, and though not a prude, does not like vulgarity or smut. She is fascinated by the reasons and motives behind the actions of others, and likes to analyse and speculate about people. She likes to talk and to feel she is of help to others. Often this sign is found in hospital welfare work and counselling. She is inclined to be a bit of a hypochondriac when all she needs for perfect health is more fresh air and exercise. She has one bad fault, that of never really listening to the other person. This is mainly because her mind, which is ruled by Mercury, has already completed what the other person is going to say. She is an organizer par excellence so that your life will be well-ordered and run to plan. She's a natural born do-gooder and improver, and health foods will figure largely on your diet, while possibly you will learn to give up cigarettes and keep your alcohol to a minimum.

To both the male and female Virgo, time is of the essence. To waste time is to waste money, and with money they are just as careful. You will have a completely dependable and competent wife, who will be faithful and loyal. However, it is just as well to remember that she, too, is self-sufficient, and could, if you took her for granted too much or played upon her trust in you, be capable of ending your association. You would then be faced with chaos where order was, and the knowledge that you had let the substance go for the shadow. For the Virgo woman has a charisma that is unique and intriguing and which lasts to her dying day.

Virgo: First Decan

If born between 24 August and 3 September you are over-fussy at times, like to be alone and do everything after due consideration. Marriage would be difficult for you, unless you were allowed a measure of freedom or isolation, as you need to be away from people to regain your balance sometimes, and people en masse almost terrify you.

Virgo: Second Decan

If born between 3 and 13 September you are the most successful Virgo, for your steady progress will be due to your thoroughness, your perfectionism, your critical faculties and your reasoning powers. Your persistence in the face of obstacles will win the day. The only thing that could hold you back is your supersensitivity.

Virgo: Third Decan

If born between 13 and 23 September you are the type who could occasionally kick over the traces and indulge in a rather lurid but secret love life. You are firm in all other respects, but possibly because the life you lead is quiet and reserved, you feel the need to prove yourself in this area.

Virgo: Lucky Features

Lucky colours:	Pale blue, pale gold and yellow, jade green
Lucky stones:	Sapphire jade, diamond and jasper
Lucky numbers:	10 for Virgo; 5 for Mercury
Lucky day:	Wednesday
Flowers:	Cornflower, lily
Tree:	Hazel-tree
Animal:	Squirrel
Birds:	Parrot, magpie
Metal:	Gold

Libra: Male

24 September to 23 October

Ruling planet:	Venus
Ruling symbol:	The Scales
Ruling sign:	Air

Libra is the sign of beauty, harmony and love. The fine finish, the attention to the nest, the good things in life, the narrowing of life down to one person are all Libran characteristics. Libra loves soft music and shared interests, although Librans have a love of solitude at times and this is very necessary to them, they have a shining quality and a loyalty that can surpass all other signs. Good food (and often both the male and female subjects are good cooks) and harmonious, elegant surroundings are also necessary because they really pay attention to the setting, and are miserable in drab surroundings and sick if involved in discord and worries.

They hate noise, confusion, loudmouthed people, domineering types and arguments. Often, because of their peculiar and particular way of seeing both sides, they will argue for the underdog or the other view, even if they themselves don't approve or share it. They like to repay their debts, either in hospitality, money or kindness, and never forget kindness, yet will make many an excuse for deliberate hurt or rudeness on the part of someone they love or once loved. Tending to cling to the idealized concept too long, they hate to admit they were wrong in the estimate of someone's character.

Money to them is to be spent, on the good things of life and friends. Once they have matured they learn to balance and discard in their lives and also learn to give their loved ones more personal freedom, but this does not usually happen until they have experienced many a scorching experience in love. Charming and warm, they seldom become bitter and often have a naïve or childlike charm that stays with them throughout life, protecting them or bringing them protection from earthier and more powerful signs. They have a habit of procrastinating, particularly if the issue is unpleasant. They are precise and time conscious and need to have their life plan worked out early in life so that they do not dither. Refined and elegant of mind, they are attracted to the arts, to poetry, music, drama and ballet. Politeness is one of their inherent traits, and people often mistake this for weakness.

Libra men are seldom serious sportsmen, and Libra ladies are usually found displaying their charms near the water or the tennis court, mainly because that's where the men would be. Libra men will often be found in a women's milieu, such as fashion designing, hairdressing and beauty schools, and because of the orderliness inherent in their natures, can also be found at universities, in government, architecture and teaching.

As they are always seeking love with a capital 'L', they appear to be flirts, but it's not that at all, it's just that they have to find the ideal. Libra men like soft appealing women, with modulated pleasant voices and ladylike manner. Arguments, as we know, make him ill, but intelligent discussions on an abstract level are his meat and drink. He tests at first, and will be slow to bring to the boil, because he knows his own weaknesses and wants to see if the mental companionship and the rapport is lasting between you before he commits himself, for to him the physical union is sacred and a sublime expression of all the other facets of love, and he knows that warmth and affection to him are the bricks and sex the cement between them.

He loves order and quiet at home, hates monotony and loves to be in your company so much you would have to let him see sometimes it is good for you both to get away from each other for short intervals. He never minds having a career wife, in fact, the more artistic the career the more proud and helpful he will be.

Libra: Female

The Libra woman, more than the male, and more than any other sign in the Zodiac, thinks of the other person before herself. Her first interest is love, and her partner, then her children and her home in that order. All Librans are good dancers and most are unusually attractive. The Libra female can be flirtatious, loves parties, people, drinking and dancing and in particular loves compliments upon her appearance, which is usually stunning. She can keep her career and her personal life in separate pockets, but a love affair that is going badly will often slow her up and put her off stride. She has a lot of strength under that decorative exterior, and cannot abide dogmatic narrow-thinking people, and shrinks from the bullying 'Me Tarzan, you Jane' approach.

Time has little meaning for this lady, but she does not like sudden changes of plan. Her life must have security, and often she can make errors by not allowing herself to be a little more spontaneous. Her politeness makes her punctual, even though it is a great effort, and also carries over into her married life. She would not dream of asking you where you have been, if you came home late, but would wait for you to tell her, nor would she open your mail or pry into your secret thoughts. She finds it hard to express her innermost thoughts and worries and needs to express her aims and thoughts more directly to avoid misunderstanding with her partner.

Unfortunately, the Libran woman seems to be attracted to the type who loves romance, the show-off type, the exciting adventurer, and as lies are abhorrent to her, she usually endures one shocking hurtful break-up of an idealized love affair before she learns to look below the surface. When she does choose happily, the man who captures this prize is a lucky man indeed. He has a partner in the true sense of the word who will build him an oasis in the desert, and will help him attain his highest ambitions.

Libra: First Decan
If born between 24 September and 3 October you are the more practical Libran. Music will play a big part in your life. You will be more time oriented than the rest of your sign and could run a business which catered in some way to beauty or the arts, such as music teaching, dress designing, managing a music or a dress shop, interior decorating, or being a colour consultant. You are less lazy then the other decans.

Libra: Second Decan
If born between 4 October and 13 October you could easily become too preoccupied with material possessions and worship your household goods too much. This is the artistic decan, which gives great physical and personal charm and loads of talent, but also the ability to ruthlessly discard people when the going becomes unpleasant, or change horses in midstream when things become too frustrating.

Libra: Third Decan
If born between 13 October and 23 October this decan gives its natives the concept of service and the love of people. Its natives are gregarious, love reading, are born teachers, a little too fond of pleasure and alcohol, and tend to put themselves last too often, so that they become doormats for their loved ones. They will run from a fight, as all Librans, but if cornered can be scathing and strong, but hate themselves afterwards for both their lack of control and their spleen.

Libra: Lucky Features
Lucky colours: Sea green, sea blue, brown, purples

Lucky stone:	Opal
Lucky number:	3
Lucky days:	Wednesdays and Saturdays
Flowers:	Daisy, violet, orchid
Trees:	Apple and grape or ash-tree
Animal:	Cat
Birds:	Love-bird or canary
Metal:	Copper

Scorpio: Male

24 October to 23 November

Ruling planets:	Mars and Pluto
Ruling symbols:	The Eagle and Scorpion
Ruling sign:	Water

This is the most inflammable sign of the Zodiac. The unforgettable people. The best and the worst of all the signs, it has been said. Proud, vain, usually either good-looking or intriguing, with an air of command, like Leos they never take a back seat. Scorpios are power orientated, straight to the point, often with little humour, strong, suspicious, shrewd judges of character. They can often underestimate one type by mistaking gentleness for weakness. They can be ruthless with adversaries and never forget a slight, and will wait years to repay someone in a fitting and similar way for an injury. They can be destructive in their emotions, yet as lovers, almost irresistible; highly sexed, with great willpower and stamina. Scorpio is not a man to trifle with.

They never tell all, and much of their nature is a mystery, which only adds to the allure. They can often be picked out of a crowd by their springy walk and the piercing quality of their gaze. They make good detectives, for their curiosity is insatiable and they probe beneath the surface, for both information and other people's weaknesses. Their judgement of people is partly intuitive, for this is one of the Occult signs. Scorpios are a contradiction even to themselves, for they, like the Scorpion, can sting themselves quite often, and lose friends and things dear to them by their own actions. A highly developed Scorpio man would be cultured, philosophic, almost mediumistic, but beware of incurring the enmity of the lower type Scorpio male.

Scorpios will be found often in surgery, laboratories (they never give up an objective, so they make good investigators), engineering, politics, and even in the Church (for their mystical side is strong), and in law (for their inherited 'eye for an eye' attitude makes them gravitate to the courts).

The Scorpio does everything intensely. He really runs risks in his kind of fierce sport, usually with the elements, for many are avid boating and sailing enthusiasts or may climb mountains as a challenge. Challenge is the operative word, if you are trying to make the grade with a Scorpio you have just met. Be careful not to antagonize him too much, or the experience will be abrasive; but challenge him a little, at the same time letting him know you are really attracted and admire him. Scorpios, like Leos, have enormous vanity, but with one difference; Scorpio can tell if you are not sincere much quicker than Leo because of his inbuilt psychic radar. Although he is intense with an aura of violence around him, the same sort of love would probably destroy the best in him, and he is more attracted, as a lasting relationship, to a calmer, saner kind of relationship.

The secretive side of Scorpio, the inarticulateness, and the lack of attention to details could irritate some other signs. His loyalty is so intense that he considers criticism of his ways a disloyalty for he expects you to accept him in total, and will seldom make an effort to change for anyone; so that, if you finally succeeded with your Scorpio you would have to be an expert at managing and organizing without appearing to criticize. His biggest fault is his jealousy and suspicion, so you would have to be prepared to have eyes for him only and never, never compare him, to his detriment, with anyone else. His superb constitution will demand large meals, plenty of activity, lashings of sex and your constant presence behind him in the upward climb. In return, he will fend for you magnificently, and give you the best in life he can possibly give, for he does not believe in half measures, it's all or nothing.

Scorpio: Female

She doesn't have to gild the lily, like the women of Taurus or Cancer. She may not even have the fashion sense that the women of Leo and Libra have, but she has something, age old, so that when she walks into a room all male eyes swivel to her and all female mouths tighten a little. She is passionate but selective, self-assured and poised, dignified and restrained (unless her famous temper gets out of control), sensual and sensitive. Her psychic powers are very strong, and she draws people to her like a magnet because she is interested in finding out all there is to know about humanity.

Usually either a keen fitness addict, or a health foods fan, she is always conscious of the physical health's effect on the mental health, and admires people who are active and athletic and who do not waste their human potential in any way. Her likes are strong; like the male counterpart, she takes no half measures. If she finds a man, he becomes her world, to the exclusion of everything else. This possession can become a little frightening and smothering, for she is oriented towards him completely and turns her back on the world outside.

Never worried by convention, she works by her own laws and moves and gets to the heart of matters far quicker than other signs. She is a perfectionist, and does everything well, if it is important to her, for then it is a challenge or even a dogfight. Women sense that she constitutes a threat to the ordered scheme of things, and she, in turn, regards them all as rivals; so that most Scorpio women prefer to make friends among the male sex since the wiles and lures attributed to femininity are foreign to this woman.

While they are still playing at little girls, the Scorpio woman has reached the ultimate femininity, and regards most other women with slight contempt and not a little bewilderment. She is intensely suspicious and when roused, can be vindictive and destructive, but provided you give her no reason to doubt your loyalty and affection, you can have a wonderful life. But if you do injure her, remember her motto 'take what you want the good God says, but pay for it'. For you will pay for it, even if she has to wait twenty years. You need an asbestos suit to deal with this lady, at times, but the good times would well make up for them.

Scorpio: First Decan

If born between 24 October and 2 November, you are rather detached and sometimes seem to be on another plane. You are restrained and modest, surprisingly enough, and for a Scorpio, you are uncharacteristic in that you could be influenced by others rather easily.

Scorpio: Second Decan

If you were born between 3 and 12 November you are the sunny natured Scorpio, often blunt and tactless, but also friendly, open and gregarious. Your only fault is that you tend to trust friends a little too easily as you judge them by your own standards, and will often be hurt when betrayed by someone in whom you have put a lot of trust.

Scorpio: Third Decan

If born between 13 and 23 November then you are the strongest of the Scorpios. You are a contained bundle of atomic energy whose ambition knows no bounds and whose energy, persistence, intelligence and intensity will eventually bring you everything you aim for. Your determination is as strong as the strongest Taurean, and you can be quite ruthless in stepping on people as you climb up the ladder.

Scorpio: Lucky Features

Lucky colours:	Dark red and crimson, purple
Lucky stones:	Topaz, ruby
Lucky number:	4
Lucky day:	Wednesday
Flower:	Tiger-lily
Trees:	Heather or chestnut
Bird:	Eagle
Metal:	Bronze

Sagittarius: Male

23 November to 21 December

Ruling planet:	Jupiter
Ruling symbol:	The Archer
Ruling sign:	Fire

Sagittarian males are, from the female point of view, the most satisfying and the most exasperating sign of the Zodiac. They make wonderful lovers and friends, are warm, demonstrative, affectionate, uninhibited, highly principled and sometimes romantic. But when they want to, they can also be extremely difficult and then the other side of their nature comes into play: their unconventionality allied to devastating honesty, their willingness to sacrifice everything for freedom of thought and action, their predilection for giving advice and their hatred of possession and domination.

Sagittarians love to fight with gusto and with no holds barred and they care about humanity. They can have an uncanny sense or awareness of others and sometimes will unerringly point out weak spots in others and attack these with enjoyment. Being almost one track people when working or doing something that is important, it is possible for them to blot out day to day concerns in their immense concentration on the task in hand. Order and tidiness around the home do not interest the Sagittarian, who prefers things to be functional as well as beautiful, and who considers his home to function for him and not the convenience or approval of his friends.

His tastes are usually highly artistic but unconventional, and he expects people to accept him as he is. (This is a little hard to accept when he himself is always so full of advice for others.) However, there is seldom malice in a Sagittarian's nature, unless he is frustrated throughout his life in regard to his career or talent. Then he can tend to look for the less available qualitites in others because of his own dissatisfaction and bitterness.

They love travel, are loquacious and well informed, kind and compassionate, are open and frank about sex, so that it becomes a happy and joyous sharing, and can often through their self-honesty laugh at themselves and the ironies and incongruities of life. They have an essential refinement that somehow prohibits swearing overduly, and the smutty bawdy emphasis on sex. They are reliable and stable, extremely generous, and thoroughly nice guys.

All you have to do is either catch them under twenty or over forty, when they seem to be more vulnerable, and as fewer are born than under any other sign, it seems you will have a very hard task finding any.

Reckless sportsmen excelling in speed, they often are found in the ranks of the professional sportsmen, among airline pilots, in the navy, at the racetrack (they are horse mad) and even in gambling dens. The Sagittarian is left cold by elaborate use of cosmetics, or sophisticated hairdos. He likes his women fresh, tangy and different. Not for him the shy little violet, or the stay-at-home with nothing to talk about. The more interesting you and your job are the more interested he will be. To find a common interest, talk to him of travel or sport, or music, which is another of his loves, but keep in mind that these creatures are nervous and tricky, and are just as likely to take off into the blue, for the thought of permanence really terrifies them. If you do manage to capture one, then go very quietly for a few years. Try not to rub in the 'togetherness'. Never question him regarding his friendship if you are wise. He is quite capable of having just that with another woman, but it would never impinge on your relationship. He is interested in partnership all the way and will encourage you to have your activities and friends apart from your shared interests for he likes to know you are developing your own personality, as he likes to feel free to develop his own.

Sagittarius: Female

She is, like Virgo, self-sufficient, sometimes overly independent, free, generous, sharing, merry and talkative, intelligent and aware and has no desire to compete with a man, or to cling possessively. Rather, her love of personal freedom, and hatred of any form of restraint that fetters individual self-expression, makes her long for a mate, in the right sense of the word. She wants to complement and complete her man. He must have physical appeal, for she herself is a warm, passionate lady, but also there must be something for her to respect and admire about him, something interesting or alive about his work.

She is determined to the point of obstinacy at times, particularly if she has made up her mind on a course of action, and nothing in this world will prevent her. She is trusting and loyal, is a logical thinker, a great sharer of problems, and a greater dispenser of love and good cheer; love to her is something special, and the union of two people; the feeling of sharing, a very important thing in her life. The sense of being buttressed by someone else who thinks as she does and cares, really cares, is one of the cornerstones of her marriage. If, for any reason, this feeling changes, then she will ruthlessly cut out and try to start anew, later, somewhere else. She can only save when she has a definite goal, always wants to buy the best of everything, is a casual housekeeper, and usually very untidy. She rather likes the mess and muddle for it bolsters up her sense of the unexpected in life, the belief in the fairytale when like a squirrel, with its sense of hoarding, she comes across something she's put away or lost.

She is constructive in her approach, and unless embittered does not often share the male failing of sensing people's weaknesses and attacking them, but if roused on someone else's behalf can be a formidable opponent. She will never be imposed on, and has a dignity and control that allow her to gravitate naturally to positions of honour and trust on committees and community activities. She becomes physically ill after domestic quarrels and needs to get away near mountains for a period of quiet meditation every so often to recharge the batteries. She won't spoon feed her man, and in some details, life could be as catch as catch can, but in the essentials, this is the girl to have at your side.

Sagittarius: First Decan
If born between 23 November and 1 December you are are a rebel. You hate restriction or controls, love analysing and dissecting things and are bluntly honest and sometimes offensive because of this. You should always endeavour to work for yourself, or work in a profession where you are trusted and are your own boss.

Sagittarius: Second Decan
If born between 2 and 11 December you are so open you find it hard

to deceive or keep a secret. You are emotional and very independent. Discussions, particularly on philosophical or occult subjects, fascinate you, but you will talk about anything for the sake of communicating ideas. You would make a good teacher.

Sagittarius: Third Decan

If born between 12 and 21 December, you would be more concerned with humanitarian issues and could seem to be detached and indifferent. Often you are so single-minded in your search for personal fulfilment and material success, that people just appear as subsidiaries or bit players, until you have reached your goal. You have the instinctive awareness of others' failings and weak spots, and at times can cruelly expose these in order to bolster up your own sense of righteousness. However, this happens only rarely, and usually only when the subject has become bitter and disillusioned (a rare thing for the jovial Jupiter-ruled Sagittarian).

Sagittarius: Lucky Features

Lucky colours:	Purple, pink
Lucky stone:	Turquoise
Lucky number:	9
Lucky day:	Friday
Flowers:	Wallflower, carnation, dandelion
Trees:	Oak, birch
Animal:	Horse
Bird:	Swallow
Metal:	Tin

CHAPTER 2

Are Your Star Signs Compatible?

Capricorn

Capricorn with Capricorn
This could be a dull-serious rather stuffy combination. The biggest pitfall is the predilection for using others — if this happens in this partnership, one partner will move on — leaving bitterness and wounded pride behind.

Capricorn with Aquarius
This is not an easy partnership or an inspiring one. Both signs are ruled by Saturn and are rather strong on sincerity, independence and loyalty — but Aquarius is more changeable than Capricorn whose stubborness could prevent rapprochement in times of stress.

Capricorn with Pisces
This could be a very productive union, although these signs are as different as chalk and cheese. Pisces are fluid and adaptable. Capricornians find a common link in the preservation of the status quo, the familiar, the time-honoured — the safe way.

Capricorn with Aries
If both subjects are mature this can be a rewarding union — but the Capricorn will not be dominated, so that the Arian partner will have to share his aims and attitudes to make this marriage a success.

Capricorn with Taurus
A fruitful, productive, materialistic union, with lashings of worldly

success and few clashes, but when the clashes come, run for cover. The Taurean will wreck the china shop, and then forgive and forget, but the Capricorn will never give up trying to get his or her way.

Capricorn with Gemini
A different union and one which could be the attraction of opposites and only successful if both partners are mature and tolerant — or if the Gemini is the male partner.

Capricorn with Cancer
A combination giving peace, plenty, harmony, productiveness and long-lasting love, as long as the Capricorn is a man.

Capricorn with Leo
Two headstrong signs — both thinking their way is best. If one is prepared to give way, this could be a wealthy union in terms of cash and power.

Capricorn with Virgo
Particularly if the female is Virgo, this combination can make a successful partnership, resulting in prestige, power and mutual understanding.

Capricorn with Libra
Not considered to be a harmonious duo usually, but if the male is Libra and either in his forties or previously married, then I would say this would be a union *par excellence*.

Capricorn with Scorpio
This is a good fruitful combination particularly if the female is the Capricorn and a few years older than her mate. Common goals are essential or both could pull in opposite directions.

Capricorn with Sagittarius
A difficult combination with plenty of fireworks — but each respects the other's drive and strength. Both are straight-talking but the Sagittarius could object to the snobbery inherent in a Capricorn.

Aquarius

Aquarius with Aquarius
This combination could mean that nothing will be achieved — or great things of humanitarian nature. It all would depend on how developed the types are.

Aquarius with Pisces
These two signs are both conscious of the great depths that lie unplumbed in each other's characters. This makes for bewilderment and perplexity. But there is great mutual attraction.

Aquarius with Aries
The Aquarian hates to feel he is possessed and dominated. Many Aquarian husbands, after years of marriage, suddenly take off for parts unknown because they can stand the mental restrictions and domination of their Arian mate not one minute longer!

Aquarius with Taurus
These two signs are on different wave lengths. Only if the Taurean is the female partner or if the Taurean husband is proud of his career wife's achievements, will this be a success.

Aquarius with Gemini
This combination is exciting. One spurs the other to new achievements and successes — and interest never lags.

Aquarius with Cancer
This can be a harmonious association, but usually only if the female is the Cancer. The rare Cancer husband who can adjust to his Aquarian wife's views and friends will have a wonderfully happy and loving marriage.

Aquarius with Leo
A wonderful physical union — and if both are tolerant and prepared to give, a wonderful combination, particularly if the woman is Aquarian.

Aquarius with Virgo
These two signs do not seem to generate great passion — but for a marriage where the partners run a business together — none to better it.

Aquarius with Libra
A lovely heady combination with all the attributes of a life-long love affair, so long as the Libra partner does not covet beauty and comfort to the point of selfishness.

Aquarius with Scorpio
The Scorpio partner may turn out to be too strong, fiery and dominating, stifling the Aquarian's love of freedom.

Aquarius with Sagittarius
This could be a risk — but also is one of the best combinations of all for Aquarius, provided the Aquarian learns to say 'I'm sorry' and the Sagittarian learns there are other points of view.

Aquarius with Capricorn
Capricorn would tend to be restrictive and possessive — while the Aquarian disregard of established tradition could enrage the Capricorn subject.

Pisces

Pisces with Pisces
A dreamy cloud-seven duo which will need lots of cash, so that a housekeeper and secretary can be hired to attend to the practical every-day details of living.

Pisces with Aquarius
The meeting of the minds — the fascination of the hidden — the occult — inexplicable new ideas — all these are part of the attraction of these two signs — but the Pisces can become too submerged, too quiescent, and irritate the Aquarian.

Pisces with Aries
These two signs have very little in common — unless the Pisces is content to be Little Sir Echo — and agree with everything the Arian says. Aries always feels Pisces is indecisive and vague and becomes irritated.

Pisces with Taurus
There will be little intellectual attraction between these two, but affection and friendship could be strong. The basicness of Taurus would make Pisces both attracted by Taurus's love of security and comfort and irritated by his commonsense practicality.

Pisces with Gemini
Although one will be a constant mystery to the other, these two signs could agree to disagree, although there could be basic differences through lack of organization and logic on the part of the Pisces.

Pisces with Cancer
This could be a life-time partnership although there will have to be one leader in the combination or nothing will get done and life will be lived on a very emotional plane.

Pisces with Leo
This combination could succeed, particularly if the female is Pisces, as she will admire the drive, honesty and strength of Leo, and possibly the deviousness and mystery of the Piscean will serve to keep the Leo interested and puzzled.

Pisces with Virgo
This is the attraction of opposites and could only last if both types were developed and tolerant. There could be much drama and many high spots, but this combination would be better for a short term as neither gives the other anything lasting.

Pisces with Libra
If neither is over-ambitious or highly gifted artistically this combination would be very happy, idealistic, emotional and have moments of great

beauty. However, if one or the other has a compulsion to succeed in the arts, this union would prove frustrating and unproductive as both these signs need someone behind them with drive and determination. Libra tends to get lazy and selfish, Pisces tend to overreach themselves and need to be held down to the task in hand.

Pisces with Scorpio
There is a wonderful attraction between these two signs. One tends to complement the other. Scorpio must dominate and Pisces can be passive and soothe the savage breast of the Scorpio like music, although he often uses devious means to gain ends.

Pisces with Sagittarius
A doubtful union, depending upon what the chief interests of the Sagittarian are. If he or she is mystically inclined then there could be a basis for communion, but it is quite possible, since both are self-contained signs that lead an inner life all of their own, that they can both live harmoniously without ever delving very closely into the other's character.

Pisces with Capricorn
If the Piscean is a woman, this combination would be rewarding — as she would enjoy the security a Capricorn male could give. However, if the Piscean is a male, his dreaminess might irritate an ambitious Capricorn female.

Aries

Aries with Aries
A surprisingly compatible union, if all other factors, such as backgrounds, age and material standards are satisfactory. There will be loyalty and lots of excitement, but one will have to knuckle under to the other, or they have to work out areas in which each is dominant.

Aries with Aquarius
There is the interest of pioneering new ideas, and a similar independence, but there will be little relaxation and peace. Aries,

however, could become too domineering and impatient with Aquarius.

Aries with Pisces
There is the constant attraction of opposites but the Arian would always consider the Pisces slow and dreamy, and would never understand the Piscean fully.

Aries with Taurus
Not a successful combination this. Two strong, stubborn signs which could get along well on the surface, but when conflict arises, the sparks will fly. Taurus certainly needs material security but also needs to retain dignity, and Aries could never resist the chance to crow when the victor. Taurus never forgets an injury to his pride and dignity.

Aries with Gemini
If an Aries female, this combination could succeed. Neither holds a grudge, and although quarrels could be frequent, life would be very rewarding provided the interests in common were maintained.

Aries with Cancer
Aries could easily annihilate Cancer in this relationship. Not good for permanency. There could be too little common ground.

Aries with Leo
If the male is Arian this combination would be bound to be successful, although it could work very well the other way around, provided that neither tried to dominate, but worked on a partnership basis.

Aries with Virgo
This combination could work if the male were Aries and there were a mental closeness and a similarity of interests. Aries could become irritated with Virgo's fussy attention to details and could be dampened by Virgo's common sense.

Aries with Libra
Opposites can have a magnetic attraction or a like repulsion! This combination would be good only for a short period. Aries loves a fight.

Libra retreats. Aries loves freedom, Libra likes to cling.

Aries with Scorpio
This combination could have much dash and fire, but Scorpio could quench Aries who is straightforward and forgives but never forgets a deceit, while Scorpio waits to repay a slight or criticism. There would be competitiveness, for these signs have a lot in common, and are both demanding and ruthless.

Aries with Sagittarius
The best combination of all provided both parties are strongly individual, and neither tries to possess the other. Here, the competitive element is lost in the mutual appreciation of each other's qualities, and both can co-operate freely.

Aries with Capricorn
Two hidebound signs, and definitely strong ones. An Arian woman could be repelled by the calculation of Capricorn, and abhor the kind of waiting game and status seeking that Capricorn revels in. Capricorn could become impatient with the enthusiasm and frightened by the challenge of the unknown which stimulates Aries into exploration and innovation.

Taurus

Taurus with Taurus
Too steady to be interesting. Yet this combination could achieve material prosperity, and if both are allied with music or the arts, such as singing or sculpture, it could mean a balanced existence, and much mutual give and take.

Taurus with Aquarius
The Aquarian would be too casual about material things and too impersonal in affairs of the heart, to make Taurus happy. Aquarius would resent Taurus's possessiveness, and Taurus would be bewildered by Aquarius because of his unpredictability and love of freedom.

Taurus with Pisces
There will be little intellectual attraction between these two, but affection and friendship could be strong. The basicness of Taurus would make Pisces both attracted by the security and comfort and irritated by the commonsense practicality. Taurus would keep the Piscean's ambitions down to earth and practical.

Taurus with Aries
This could only succeed if the woman were the Taurean partner. But how the sparks would fly! Both would have to be mature people — and learn to say 'I'm sorry' often.

Taurus with Gemini
A rarely successful combination, but it could work, particularly if the Taurean is artistically gifted in some way. Then the Gemini would respect both the talent and the persistence of Taurus, and provided the Taurean was tolerant and allowed the Gemini to stray slightly sometimes, the Gemini partner would give support and bring new ideas and techniques to the more conventional Taurean.

Taurus and Cancer
The common ground here is the love of food and material security. Both are emotional and affectionate, traditional in outlook, love their home, and Cancer, the giver, would find Taurus undemonstratively grateful and loyal. There would be few high spots in this association: it would be quiet and serene. The only drawback is Cancer's supersensitivity and Taurus's misleadingly brusque inarticulate exterior.

Taurus with Leo
Physically this could be a great union, and if both partners are spiritually undeveloped, or relatively simple people, it could be a happy marriage; however, both signs wish to be boss, and Leo's quick rages are forgotten in an hour whereas Taurus does a slow boil and erupts, often with fatal consequences, particularly if he feels he is taken for granted, a habit that Leo has with most of his friends. Taurus will appreciate Leo and give him an audience, but who will appreciate Taurus?

Taurus with Virgo
Sexy, this could be a wonderful partnership. However, if the Virgoan were not strongly physical, Taurus would in time be repelled by the coldness and self-preoccupation of his partner, for his nature needs warm love like a flower needs sun, and to him the physical side of love is the best way of expressing what he feels.

Taurus with Libra
If the Taurean were the breadwinner then this could be wonderful. Libra can manage Taurus and create beauty and harmony in the surroundings which are essential to both. The relationship would have lots of affection and warmth, and Taurus could learn finesse in matters pertaining to sex from Libra, who in turn would feel protected and cherished.

Taurus with Scorpio
Basically a physical attraction: both are strong, stubborn signs, with a tendency to possessiveness, jealousy and suspicion. There would have to be much in common plus a mutual trust before this relationship would work. Scorpio could destroy the less devious Taurus.

Taurus with Sagittarius
A difficult combination, but opposites attract, and although Sagittarius is a wanderer, with a tolerance and wisdom which Taurus natives cannot share, this could be a workable combination. The sex drive would be strong, and Sagittarius could enjoy the challenge.

Taurus with Capricorn
Serious types both of these natives, with a love of security and a reverence for the past; this union would be most satisfying for two people who are patient, ambitious, materialistic, home-loving and earthy. There would be very little frivolity connected with this alliance.

Gemini

Gemini with Gemini
What fun! This combination would never be static and probably never

last. One would never give the other the chance to air opinions or have his say. As a business partnership, particularly something pertaining to mental pursuits, this could be wildly successful, also with fashion and publishing. But as a marriage, there would be too little peace, too much tension, and health and nerves would crack up.

Gemini with Aquarius
An exciting, adventurous existence, and a great mental attraction as well as a physical bond.

Gemini with Pisces
This could be quite a good partnership, and also good for mutual creative activities.

Gemini with Aries
This union would need to develop outside interests in common. An Aries man could become impatient with a Gemini woman's lack of purpose.

Gemini with Taurus
A difficult combination — but if the Gemini is a male he could get a lot of help and support from his practical, level-headed Taurus partner.

Gemini with Cancer
This union would entail a lot of tolerance, sacrifice and hard work to make it a success. However, if the Cancer makes an extra effort to share Gemini's interests, the different moods of the Cancer can intrigue Gemini and keep him interested. However, the sentimental streak in Cancer almost repels Gemini, so that would have to be kept hidden.

Gemini with Leo
Geminis are restless, mercurial and always on the go — they love variety, surprises and nearly always have a current craze which they will drop as suddenly as they picked it up. In a partner, they look above all for understanding and sympathy. But Leo, vain, jealous and egocentric, would find it hard to take second place.

Gemini with Virgo
This is only successful for short term relationships. The unreliability of Gemini could drive Virgo mad, while the fussiness and narrowness of Virgo could lead Gemini into wordy sarcastic battles. Unless there were strong mental interests in common, which could balance the lack of strong emotional contact in both these signs, this union would fail.

Gemini with Libra
A very good pairing. There is a mutual compatibility which leads to mental pursuits in common, shared ideas and love of hospitality and the arts. Libra's sentimentality could irritate Gemini, but their innate fairness and balance, their love of harmony and peace, could soothe and make whole.

Gemini with Scorpio
There is a lot to be learned from each other in this combination. They are so different that the union could falter on the rock of Gemini's love of freedom and Scorpio's suspicious jealousy, while there would be inequality in the emotional response that could sour Scorpio.

Gemini with Sagittarius
A good combination, but Sagittarius would need to temper his blunt truth-telling. Both are freedom loving, active mentally and physically and both are adaptable and tolerant. Gemini's exaggerations might irk the Sagittarian, while the Sagittarian's logic might antagonize and confuse the Gemini.

Gemini with Capricorn
These two do not appreciate each other's qualities. The chopping and changing of the Gemini could irritate the Capricorn, while the status seeking, the snobbishness and the using quality in Capricorn could alienate the Gemini.

Cancer

Cancer with Cancer
This union will be a very quiet one; however, if both have the same

goals in life, they will pull together but both have a tendency to live in the past, and tend to let the present pass by. There is much sensitivity and understanding in this relationship.

Cancer with Aquarius
The detachment and impersonal attitude of the Aquarian should upset the Cancer who is much more emotionally tied to people, while the Aquarian's love of freedom, and the Cancer's need to cling and his sustained emotional demands will in time tire and bore the Aquarian.

Cancer with Pisces
This combination, emotionally, has much in common; some astrologers would assert that these two signs would possess the necessary mutual sympathy to make a lasting union. However, practical objectives and everyday living could become confused with the lack of logic and effective planning.

Cancer with Aries
Aries could easily annihilate Cancer in this relationship. Not good for permanency. There could be too little common ground.

Cancer with Taurus
A very successful union — resulting in a comfortable home and love of family — although it could be a little unadventurous and hidebound.

Cancer with Gemini
If the Cancer is female there is a better chance of this marriage succeeding, as long as she is prepared to make changes and possible moves in their married life — which is difficult for Cancer, who loves to be settled.

Cancer with Leo
In the right circumstances, this can be a perfect union for when they find the right person, Cancer subjects are loyal to the last. They are perfectionists, so happiness may not come easily, but in strong extrovert Leo they should find an ideal partner on whom they can lavish their attention and affection.

Cancer with Virgo
This could be a successful combination because Cancer is slow and sure and is himself sincere and conscientious, so he would appreciate the dedication and the perfection and fastidiousness of the Virgo nature. The only failing could be in that the Cancer would not receive the affection and the security that his nature desires from the rather aloof and detached and cold Virgo.

Cancer with Libra
This is a difficult union in many ways and, although both are peace-loving, and avoid discord, Cancer's emotionalism could easily offend the finely balanced Libra, while Libras may selfishly allow Cancer's protective instinct to pamper and spoil them.

Cancer with Scorpio
This could be a good union: there would be a strong intuitive tie here. Both are highly psychic signs and highly emotional. Communication could be difficult. The Cancer could soothe the Scorpio, but should emotions get out of hand, the Cancer would suffer greatly.

Cancer with Sagittarius
This relationship gives a very close friendship at the best. One side is a wanderer and one is a home-lover and Sagittarians will not be owned even mentally, which is a fault with Cancers because they tend to cling in every way and want to share both mental and physical pursuits.

Cancer with Capricorn
These are opposite signs and opposites often attract, and this is usually a good combination. But the lack of warmth and the one-directional aim of Capricorn could repel the sensitive Cancer, who could feel neglected. Possibly the most successful union would occur if the Capricorn were older and male and the Cancer were younger and female.

Leo

Leo with Leo
Who gives in to whom? These two could destroy each other in the

battle for supremacy and attention, if both are true types. Better keep it a friendship.

Leo with Aquarius
A physically rewarding union but the detachment of the Aquarian, and the self-possession of the Leo, could result in a sterile partnership. The very difference in attitude could interest both but there would be little understanding of each other.

Leo with Pisces
Another puzzle for both parties. Leo may never know how conniving and secretive Pisces is (particularly if the Pisces is a female). He would not approve, but be constantly intrigued, while the Pisces would be attracted by the straightforward no-nonsense attitude and the protection and security the male Leo gives.

Leo with Aries
A Leo male would find an Arian female gives him the necessary drive — but his need for flattery would not be met. Arians do not suffer fools gladly and are often impatient with over-confident people.

Leo with Taurus
A better combination if the male is the Leo. Good for material wealth, but these are two very strong and stubborn signs.

Leo with Gemini
The danger here is that Leo's vanity will suffer because Gemini does not have time to pander to it all the time, and his pride will be hurt because his superior attitude and generally noble air could make Gemini resort to ridicule. However, this could be a strong combination because both must be up and doing and neither suffers from an inhibiting inferiority complex. The one thing that Leo would find incomprehensible, is the lightness with which Gemini regards some loyalties.

Leo with Cancer
This is a good combination — particularly if the male is Leo. He will

have the admiring audience he craves.

Leo with Virgo
There is little chance of this union being a success due to the lack of sympathy and common attitudes and aims. Unless the male is the Leo and the Virgo female can be content with her subordinate position, then it is better as a business partnership.

Leo with Libra
Libra's inherent good taste and balance could be offended by the extravagance of Leo's character, his hyperbole and his conceit. However, this could be one of the most satisfactory unions for Leo, particularly if the male were Leo, or the career person of the partnership were the Leo.

Leo with Scorpio
Another wonderful union, but Scorpio hasn't the sunniness or the generosity or tolerance of Sagittarius. The Scorpio would have to curb his inherent cruelty and refrain from puncturing Leo's enthusiasm, otherwise it could become a holocaust.

Leo with Sagittarius
This can be a marvellous combination. Leo, at his best, is generous and tolerant; Sagittarius is even more generous and even more tolerant and philosophic. They are both outgoing and honest, with lashings of affection. So as long as Sagittarius thinks Leo's vanity is endearing, and Leo allows for the Sagittarian's desire for individual expansion and personal freedom, this would be an ideal union.

Leo with Capricorn
Both are out for position and power, but both have different methods of seeking them. Leo could be brought down by Capricorn's cold and stern nature and lose a lot of *joi de vivre*.

Virgo

Virgo with Virgo
A splendid match. The only problem with this partnership would be the tendency to nag and find fault, while there could be the danger of conflict of family interests in the desire to serve humanity. The children could be both lonely and over-organized.

Virgo with Aquarius
This is a purely mental relationship. Aquarius would prove a puzzle to Virgo and Virgo would depress Aquarius, the unpredictable, with his ordered predictability and orthodox outlook.

Virgo with Pisces
Virgo is analytical and logical, whereas Pisces is the opposite. There could be little real communication unless Pisces really tried hard to bridge the gap.

Virgo with Aries
A moody combination which could conceivably work, but only if it is the right kind of Virgo and the right kind of Aries. The Aries, if older and male, would have to be extremely tolerant.

Virgo with Taurus
If the male is Virgo and the female Taurus this could be a physically exciting match, and a very happy one with few very high and very low spots.

Virgo with Gemini
An unlikely combination, although both are ruled by Mercury. Virgo is the stable, dark side of the star that could stifle Gemini and bring out all the defensiveness and trickery inherent in his nature.

Virgo with Cancer
This will work best if the Virgo is a male — but Cancer could feel unappreciated and shut out. However, Virgo would enjoy Cancer's love of home and artistic flair.

Virgo with Leo
This is not usually a successful partnership unless both parties have similar backgrounds, attitudes and aims.

Virgo with Libra
Virgo's set ways would rile Libra, although both signs are perfectionists. Libra is not always logical, and will never fight where he can run. Virgo rather loves a wordy battle and despises what he thinks is Libra's cowardice.

Virgo with Scorpio
This can really be a shattering experience, particularly to the Virgoan. There could be a clash of interests and wills and neither would give in.

Virgo with Sagittarius
These two are so different, it would depend on the tolerance and development of the Sagittarian to be successful. If the Sagittarian were a sailor away at sea for long periods, or with some sort of position which took him away periodically, this could be a happy union. The impulsive generosity and the love of freedom of the Sagittarian would both hurt and annoy the Virgo.

Virgo with Capricorn
A down-to-earth conservative union, which, because neither is over-emotional, would succeed as long as the Virgo does not become fed up with the selfishness of Capricorn, and Capricorn does not crave more warmth than the Virgo can give.

Libra

Libra with Libra
A lot of fun and blissful peace, but they might as well be dead for all the progress they'll make, or the knowledge they'll gain of each other. Both would be too intent on avoiding arguments and not hurting the other's feelings to really relax and live.

Libra with Aquarius
A harmonious relationship, and an exciting one. Better if the male is Aquarian and the female Libra.

Libra with Pisces
A happy mixture, but both types have to know each other well for a long time before marriage to avoid disillusionment.

Libra with Aries
The opposites attract, but Libra could be hurt badly in this combination.

Libra with Taurus
The only problem here would be if the dreamy Libran were the breadwinner. Money then could become an issue. Other way round, quite perfect.

Libra with Gemini
A good union. Libras could soothe Geminis and give them the balance which they lack. Gemini would have to be careful of that sarcastic tongue.

Libra with Cancer
These two signs do not have the same attitudes or aims. They would confuse each other. There would be so much sensitivity in the air, it would be like beautiful dreams, but there would be a nasty awakening.

Libra with Leo
An excellent combination; Libra shares Leo's enthusiasm but can restrain his impetuosity and show him the other side of the coin. The only danger is Leo's bluntness.

Libra with Virgo
Perfectionists both, this could be a rewarding union, but only if Virgo can curb his criticism and realize that Libra cannot help trying to avoid fights, but if cornered, will fight with real courage, particularly for a friend.

Libra with Scorpio
If Libra can stand the tempestuousness of Scorpio this could be a wonderful marriage. If there are shared interests and Scorpio bends a little, learning a little of Libra's tolerance, this would be very rewarding.

Libra with Sagittarius
An excellent prospect, provided that Libra understands the necessity of leaving Sagittarius unfettered and Sagittarius realizes that with Libra sharing is important, so that he gives a little.

Libra with Capricorn
These two often seem sent to discipline each other, and provided they are philosophically inclined, this can be quite successful. The sternness and self-discipline of the Capricorn can make the Libra deflated and guilty while the laziness of the Libra irritates the go-ahead Capricorn.

Scorpio

Scorpio with Scorpio
An emotionally wearing association, excellent physically, but only workable if both have exactly the same aims in life, so that there is identity and togetherness. Any competitiveness could result in a struggle for supremacy.

Scorpio with Aquarius
This would only be successful for a short period unless there was much trust and tolerance. Aquarians do not take kindly to domination.

Scorpio with Pisces
This is a terrific combination when the male is Scorpio. Pisces' deviousness is then put down to feminine wiles and the Scorpio partner is then amused, not put off by it. There is a psychic tie between these signs. Pisces soothes and Scorpio activates.

Scorpio with Aries
Not a good combination. Too much ruthlessness, love of power and fire. Scorpio could make Aries feel inferior.

Scorpio with Taurus
A physical relationship mainly, this combination would only work with lots of mutual trust and tolerance, as one is suspicious and jealous, and the other is jealous and suspicious.

Scorpio with Gemini
Not a really satisfactory relationship, because of the intensity and passion of Scorpio and the lightness and lack of emotional response in Gemini. They could learn from each other but never understand.

Scorpio with Cancer
A very good combination this, but an emotionally-based one that has little to do with reason or communication. Things would be felt or sensed instead of being reasoned out or talked about.

Scorpio with Leo
If there were mutual tolerance and co-operation these two signs could almost move the earth, but they would both have to be developed human beings to make this a partnership and not a war.

Scorpio with Virgo
The result of this pairing could be surprising. It would all depend upon who would be willing to give more than fifty per cent.

Scorpio with Libra
The Libra would have to be the giver, and extremely tolerant for this union to be really successful. The Scorpio could be one of the happiest men alive, with this kind of partner, but the other way around would spell trouble for the Libran.

Scorpio with Sagittarius
A possible combination but only if Scorpio learned to curb his jealousy and allow Sagittarius to feel free, to wander out into the world, instead of trying to create a world just for the two of them.

Scorpio with Capricorn
This combination could be extremely good. It would all depend upon

whether both parties pulled together towards some common goal.

Sagittarius

Sagittarius with Sagittarius

Could be a winner. Lots of enthusiasm and communication. Sometimes the goals are unrealistic as they become carried away with excitement, and nothing gets done, while restriction and limitation sour and embitter.

Sagittarius with Aquarius

This could be a very good combination, sparking off mental interests. Both have the love of freedom and the development of the individual as a strong part of their make up, and both are unconventional types. Tolerance towards each other, however, would have to be practised, as each are highly individual definite types.

Sagittarius with Pisces

This is a doubtful combination. Neither would appreciate the other's point of view. Sagittarius, with the fear of being shackled and possessed, would give Pisces no feeling of security and belonging that this sign craves above all. The only basis for success could be a religious or mystical tie in common.

Sagittarius with Aries

This is a winning ticket! Both signs complement and see things to admire and respect in each other. They can go a long way together.

Sagittarius with Taurus

A strongly physical union but a difficult one which only time might cement. Each is so different that it would depend upon the stage of development of each partner whether one could learn from the other.

Sagittarius with Gemini

A more mental union than physical, this would require a lot of adjustment to enable it to work. Sagittarius might miss the warmth he craves, and Gemini might resent the blunt forthright handling of his pipe dreams and enthusiasms.

Sagittarius with Cancer

This could be a very successful match only if the male were Sagittarian and great care was taken not to hurt Cancer's feelings by too much blunt truth telling. There would be much love, laughter and companionship.

Sagittarius with Leo

This could work well if both signs show generosity and tolerance towards one another. Leo must not cramp Sagittarius's freedom and Sagittarius must make allowances for Leo's self-absorption.

Sagittarius with Virgo

A difficult union — better if the Sagittarian is the male partner, since Virgo's organization mania could depress the happy go lucky, outgoing, untidy Sagittarius.

Sagittarius with Libra

An excellent union. Both are interested in people, are idealistic, fun-loving and affectionate. The only things to watch would be Sagittarius's blunt honesty which could hurt the Libran, and Libra's tendency to avoid issues, which would infuriate the Sagittarian.

Sagittarius with Scorpio

A very interesting union, but an explosive one. Sagittarius has a gregarious nature; Scorpio has a possessive, explosive one. Scorpio is jealous; Sagittarius loves freedom.

Sagittarius with Capricorn

This is one of the most difficult of all. There seems to be nothing in common, nothing either would like or admire in the other, except possibly their love of truth and their determination. Sagittarius is sunny, outgoing, affectionate and tolerant, Capricorn is reserved, pessimistic, careful and narrow.

CHAPTER 3

The Health of Your Lover

Capricorn

Capricorn subjects can at times become very depressed, and in extremely adverse circumstances, can resort to drink and drugs to help them. Skin disorders, constipation, rheumatism are common ills for this native. They need a lot of sleep and must take care of the calcium intake in the body, as this sign rules the knees and the joints, while they must also ensure that they have plenty of calm restful weekends to give the necessary time to recharge the batteries. The mineral salt most necessary to Capricorn is phosphate of lime or calcium phosphate.

Aquarius

The legs, ankle bones and the circulation are ruled by this sign. The bones are often brittle and the circulation poor. Eating habits can be irregular and the meals hurried but this is often balanced by the fact that this sign is a natural for health food diets and could obtain necessary vitamins that way. Rheumatism, colds and bronchitis can be a health hazard and there is the danger of electric shocks. However, calcium foods, plenty of fresh air plus warmth in winter (for they really feel the cold and need good warming foods), will keep this subject well and happy. The birthsalt needed for Aquarius is sodium chloride.

Pisces

This sign is the ruler of feet, toes, nerves, lymphatic glands and often suffers from liver troubles, blood disorders, gout, dropsy and anaemia. Because of this predilection for catching colds easily, he should have fish and oil products, plenty of vitamin C and lots of steak. Not an outdoor type, he needs exercise and rest in equal proportions to prevent him from gaining overweight and also to give his nerves a rest. He should never live far from the sea. His mineral salt is ferum phosphate or phosphate of iron.

Aries
The sign ruling the head, Aries natives often suffer from headcolds, fevers, asthma, migraine, as well as burns and injuries to the face and head, concussion, injuries to the eyes and apoplexy. Their eyesight often fails them as they grow older. As these natives need no extra stimulation and should neither smoke nor drink, an ideal diet for them would be fish, salads and fresh fruit. They must have fresh air and exercise to enable them to keep their balance, for their nerves are pitched to an intensity through their driving force and ambition, and if their aims are frustrated for long periods, tension can cause high blood-pressure, heart attacks and nervous breakdowns. The mineral birthsalt for this sign is kali phos or potassium phosphate.

Taurus
This sign rules the throat, gullet, larynx, and vocal chords. Their weakness spot is the throat, but many suffer from bronchitis, tonsilitis, quinsy, catarrh and also kidney trouble in later life. The Taurean seldom does things by halves and tends to drink and smoke too much through sociability more than from a genuine liking for these things. Sensitive to atmosphere, music can almost make this native whole again, if sick. Self indulgent and loving food, they must discipline themselves out of starchy pastries and sweet foods. Their birth mineral is sulphate of sodium or nat sulph.

Gemini
This sign rules the shoulders, hands, arms, fingers, blood, lungs and respiratory system. Because he is always on the go both physically and mentally this sign needs coddling to keep the nervous and physical boilers stoked. Bronchitis and rheumatism can be a health hazard, and all troubles pertaining to the nerves. The Gemini subject should always get lots of sleep and this with particular emphasis on fresh air while he is sleeping. He needs lots of calm and quiet periods, and should eat more light snacks, possibly six a day, rather than three heavy meals.

Exercise of a gentle nature should be a must every day to keep the joints supple so that rheumatism will not be severe. The birth mineral for Gemini is kali mur, or chloride of potassium.

Cancer
Breast, stomach, digestive organs come under this sign. Bronchitis, lung troubles, colds and rheumatism can dog this subject, while accidents to the ribs are common in younger subjects, and digestive troubles and stomach ulcers in older Cancerians. This native should have lots of sea foods, rich in iodine, kelp tablets and shun alcohol, as they are prone to addiction. Cancer subjects, like Taureans, are affected by their environment, so the surroundings must always be pleasant and harmonious to soothe the nervous system. The birth mineral for this subject is fluoride of lime or calcarea flurica.

Leo
This sign rules the upper part of the back and the spine and heart. Anaemia is also often present, and there is the danger of high blood-pressure and heart trouble. Usually longlived, they have one fault, that of bolting their food while under the stress of emotion. They are easily stimulated and must learn to take everything in moderation. They need sexual stimulus, for they are magnificently endowed with sexual energy and can become morbid or ill if alone and unattached for long periods. They need people around them and are never happy unless they have someone around to love and impress. They should eat such foods as parsley, strawberries and olives for iron, and should cut down their intake of coffee, tea and alcohol. Their birth mineral is magnesium phosphate.

Virgo
Rules the head, eyes, lower spine and abdominal regions. This native can suffer from colic, constipation, colitis, indigestion and dysentery. Longlived and usually in good health, they are so intensely aware of people and are ruled by order and routine so absolutely, that should their life or relations with others become chaotic, Virgos' nerves will go to pieces. He is often a reformer against alcohol and smoking, and yet has within him the tendency to crave drugs or drink. He can become

a hypochondriac and a compulsive pill taker, and also, if disturbed, a compulsive eater, so that he has to watch his weight. For good health they must have a calm existence with quiet surroundings and no money troubles. The birth mineral is potassium sulphate or kali sulph.

Libra
This sign rules the kidneys, the skin and the lumbar region. They are often lacking in minerals such as sodium, phosphorus and iron, and can suffer from both catarrh and chronic anaemia. They should not have overmuch alcohol and fresh air is important to them. Like Cancer and Taurus, they are affected by their surroundings and can be made ill by either drab and dreary conditions sustained for too long, or excessive monotony. Colour will always make them feel uplifted, music is another remedy and the best of all is the sea. They should live near both trees and water to be ideally happy. The birth mineral is sodium phosphate.

Scorpio
This sign rules the generative and urinary organs and pelvic cage. Usually physically strong, the nervous system will work on the physical system to bring this native down. They, like Taureans, only more so, tend to go to extremes, so must be warned against excessive smoking and drinking and going for long periods without sufficient sleep. They can suffer from arthritis and rheumatic complaints in later life. If they have worked out a philosophy to inure them against the stresses of daily living, these natives will enjoy almost perfect health. It is inaction and frustration that will impair their magnificent vitality. Most Scorpios are young in mind and do not intend to grow old, and because of this they retain their youthful appearance long after their youth is gone. The birth mineral is calcium sulphate.

Sagittarius
This sign rules the hips, arteries, nerves and thighs. This native needs regular exercise all his life to promote circulation and has to be especially careful to take cleansing foods regularly so that the bloodstream is kept pure. Otherwise they will suffer such things are catarrh, bronchitis and nasal troubles. Emotional under the surface, these emotions can

be dangerous to his health if not controlled by the mind, and can shatter his nerves, particularly if he feels restricted, caged or hindered by circumstances. His sense of individual freedom is so strong that he will go to enormous lengths to protect it. Another type is susceptible to his surroundings, and gloom and pessimism can make this particular native ill, as will quarrels and criticism. They are often accident prone, particularly the legs and thighs. Their birth mineral is silica.

CHAPTER 4

Find Your Lover's Number

Primary or Character Numbers

The ancient Hebrews, from a set of beliefs called the 'Kabbala' handed down by traditions and practice, believed that certain numbers had certain associations with their alphabet, and in this way they practised the interpretation of names.

The Ancient Egyptians believed in the power and significance of numbers and used them as divinatory aids. The philosophers of Ancient Greece believed that numbers possessed a certain power of their own, independent of their mathematical laws which in their essence were pure numbers. Pythagoras, the Greek philosopher and mathematician, believed that 'numbers are the first things of all nature' and that all natural phenomena could be reduced to numerical terms.

The meanings or interpretation of the various numbers are as old as time itself, stemming from the spiritual significance primitive man visualized and assigned to each numeral. There are two systems, the primary or unit system, numbering one to nine, and the more recent Kabbala which, corresponding with the Jewish alphabet, has twenty-two numbers. We will use both to enable us to find the 'Marriage Number' and also to find the numbers which are compatible or in opposition.

Character or Primary Numbers

The meanings of the Primary numbers are as follows:

Number One

The Unity or the Monad is the symbol of the deity, the oneness of divine purpose, the hub of the universe, the Parent of the World, and the Sun. Considered to be a masculine number, because of the tradition the male was created first, those who came under the influence of this number will show the following characteristics: great tenacity, singleness of purpose, self reliance, great achievement, concentration, ingenuity, genius (occasionally), love of action and strength. People controlled by number one will be leaders, will welcome responsibilities, will be kind to those weaker than themselves, will be friendly and considerate to others but will never be happy in a subordinate position. Highly ambitious, they will tend to underestimate the character and work of others, will be stubborn, brash and over confident, scorning good advice, haughtily independent and can lapse into conceit, narrow mindedness, bigotry and intolerance.

Number Two

The Duad represents the opposites or diversity, justice and equality with its two sides, balance, harmony and brotherhood. This number is traditionally associated with the female. Those who come under the influence of this number will show: consideration to others, placidity, a love of justice, a hatred of tyranny and all forms of selfishness. People controlled by this number will go out of their way to avoid strife and discord in any form. They make friends easily because of their understanding and sympathy towards all types of characters. Their faults are mainly passive through an excess of sympathy which in turn can cause changeability and irresolution. The distaste for strife could lead to the shirking of all responsibilities while the ability to see both sides of a question and the excess sympathy may make the nature fatalistic and sometimes even indifferent. They need the strength of Number One.

Number Three

The Ternary, esteemed by the ancients as the perfect number. It is regarded as a male number, and traditionally is linked with the Trinity, as well as with matter, idea and the god of the Ancient Greeks, and the conceptions of past, present and future, and height, length and breadth. It is symbolized by the triangle, which was considered to be sacred by the Ancient Egyptians.

Those who come under this number will show fortitude and freedom, organizational flair, inventive ability, persuasive charm and business acumen. People controlled by number three will be talkative, cheerful, very adaptable to circumstances and people, exuberant and enthusiastic. They will always show optimism, and will never be affected by worry for long. Their excessive independence can often turn to indifference. Their self-engrossed attitude will offend many people, while their sudden rise to fame may have a reversal brought about by over confidence. Their impatience and lack of tenacity may be their undoing, for they need to cultivate humility, endurance and purpose to succeed.

Number Four

The quaternary of the Tetrad was thought to be the root of all things by the Ancient Greeks, as it represented fire, air, earth and water, the four winds, the four seasons and the four points of the compass. It was also considered to represent truth, and Pythagoras himself referred to the deity as the Tetrad because 'Zeus' had four letters. The number four is symbolized by the square and it stands for solidity and reality. Those who come under the influence of this number will show: stolidity, loyalty, steadiness, tenacity, honesty, conventionality, obedience and subordinance. But they have a hidden side which rebels against rules and regulations and too much red tape in governmental matters.

Those influenced by the Tetrad will show ability for performing wearisome or unpleasant tasks, a deeply faithful nature, forcefulness, willpower, abstemiousness, and a nature that will always try to find the good in others. They are slow to condemn and seldom intolerant, and could shine in social work and political reform. Practical common sense is the forte of this type, who will never shine in work requiring imagination, but this can be their failing, as they will never appreciate another person's brilliant and unconventional methods, and will shun the out-of-the-ordinary event in favour of routine. They tend to get stuck in a rut, where lack of initiative, or perhaps a lack of personal motivation or ideals will prevent them from achieving anything noteworthy in their life. They need the daring, drive and dash of Number Three to help them achieve success.

Number Five

The Quincunx or the Pentad was regarded by all the ancients as the symbol of health and fecundity, while to the Egyptians alone it also signified prosperity. It was universally linked with marriage and propagation, possibly from the union of Number Two, the female number, with the Triad, which was considered to be male. Five tapers were burned during a wedding ceremony in Ancient Rome, and five has featured as a sacred number in many religions. Its symbol is either a pyramid, a five-sided figure or the five-pointed star, which is an ancient form of the Seal of Solomon. Those who come under the influence of this number will show vivacity and versatility, courage and a strong physical constitution, romantic ardour, friendship and the ability to find pleasure in the little things of life.

Aware of the feelings of others to an extraordinary degree, they grasp the essentials of a person or a situation very quickly and can adapt themselves accordingly. They love to travel and explore the unknown and are cosmopolitan in their outlook, being able to mix easily with all strata of society. Their predilection for affairs of the heart can bring much unhappiness to others, as their affections are seldom deeply engaged. They make better friends than lovers. They can be irresponsible and lacking in concentration, and act on impulse. Often they are judged as being unreliable and untrustworthy but this is usually due to thoughtlessness and to the fact that they try to do too much at once, never completely mastering anything, and always looking for fresh fields and pastures new. They need the steadying influence of Number Two, who could counteract these faults. Their colour is violet, and this colour will strengthen the spirit and foster luck.

Number Six

The Hexagon or Hexad is represented by a six-sided figure. Also it is represented by the two interlacing triangles known as the Seal of Solomon. The Jewish people considered six a sacred number as the world was created in six days, but even heathen peoples used this double triangle to ward off evil and early Christians used it to represent the two natures of the Lord Jesus Christ. Considered to be one of the happiest numbers because it represents harmony and completion, those coming under the influence of this number will show: idealism, smooth harmony, strict honesty, kindness and care for the sick and maimed.

They are never selfish, intolerant or self indulgent and do not esteem money for its own sake but rather as a means of benefiting others. They are faithful, loving spouses, good parents and providers, although worldly wealth and position mean nothing to them, and they are happy if they are doing the kind of work that appeals to them most. They have very few unfavourable qualities. Their idealism, carried to excess, can make them appear superior to others, and their lack of concern with material success may well penalize their families. Often they will not stand up for their rights and assume an air of martyrdom, while conversely they can be too soft and kind hearted and allow people to impose upon them unnecessarily. The number six governs all shades of blue. This colour will help in all matters concerning the affections.

Number Seven

The Septenary or Septad. This is the most mysterious and interesting of the primary numbers. The Pythagoreans considered it to be sacred because it was the highest primary number which was complete in itself and could not be divided by any number but one. Ancient philosophers regarded it as the symbol of world government through the influence of the seven planets, while the Greeks and the Romans thought it to be lucky because of its connection with the different phases of the moon. The seven notes of the scale gave rise to the Philosophy of the Harmony of the Spheres, with the universe one vast musical scale. It has been significant, like the number five, in many religions ranging from the seven worlds of the Chaldeans to the seven hells and seven heavens of the Mohammedans. The Septad may be said to represent the qualities of wisdom, balance and completion, evolution and endurance. Those who come under the influence of this number will show: self discipline, fortitude, spiritual strength, isolationism, love of knowledge, love of privacy, intuition, occult power, and great mental activity.

They will be ahead of their time in their philosophy and beliefs, will love knowledge and value it above everything. Their very love of solitude can be their undoing, as they hate being forced to mix with people and become resentful and over critical as a result. Ordinary amusements are not for them, nor are they petty minded for their considerations are with the greater issues of life. However, they waste time on acquiring knowledge selfishly without any desire to impart it or make any practical use of it. They should cultivate people and learn the true worth of friendship to avoid a lonely old age, and also should develop their studies along practical lines to enable them to make some material gain and success in life. Orange is the colour of this number, or yellow and brown worn together. It rules the mind and thoughts and will aid all intellectual pursuits.

Number Eight

The Octaedron or the Ogdoad was greatly revered in Egypt. The custom seems to have stemmed from the belief that there were eight souls saved from the flood in Noah's Ark. The Egyptians always carried eight people in each boat taking part in the sacred processions, and in the Tarot cards, the symbology of which comes in part from the Ancient Egyptians' occult writings, the figure eight is used in headdresses denoting wisdom. Regarded as the first cube of mathematicians, and being the highest of the even primary numbers, it signifies balance, reality and strength. Those who come under the influence of this number will be extremely practical and will show organising ability and business sense, particularly in that sphere which calls for quick decisions, patience and authority. They have all the qualities of Number Four people but in greater measure, giving them a greater will to succeed and greater determination.

They have no time for the esoteric, but can be deeply religious, yet remain with their feet firmly on the ground at all times, and lose patience with laziness, inefficiency and day dreaming. They are prudent and resent anyone trying to take advantage of their undoubted kind nature, and can be analytical and shrewd in their judgements of people. They are not the type to fall passionately in love, but they can give a life time of loyalty and steady affection which creates its own security. Their lack of imagination can make them blunt at times, and they can annoy others by their refusal to concede that there may be other dimensions than the practical and material plane. They must learn to have more faith and be less domineering if they wish to succeed with other people, and also to try to broaden their views and rid themselves of the destructive intolerance they can display. A Number Five person could help them in this way. Eight rules the colour grey, which will foster all business concerns and anything requiring administration or organization.

Number Nine

The Nonagen or the Ennead was thought by many of the ancients to be perfection and concord and completely limitless. This came from the peculiar mathematical properties of nine, and was called Concord because it unites all the other numbers into one and perfection because the pre-natal period of development is nine months. The Romans considered this a special number. Market days were called Noveninae as they were held every nine days, and among other references Lars Porsena swore to nine Gods. The Jewish people believed that Jehovah came down to the earth nine times, and many secret societies and Kabbalistic rites incorporate the number nine. Those who come under this number show: perfectionism, discretion, great intellect, understanding, a leaning towards logic, philosophy, fine arts, and martial pursuits.

They know how to utilize their knowledge and are equipped with brilliant minds. Kind and willing to help others succeed they never take a mean advantage of anyone. Their thoughts and actions are ruled by honesty and consideration for others. They make fine sympathetic friends because of their understanding, and although they live to a set of high principles, they do not seem to judge others or feel superior to them. This is the number of genius, like Number One, but they lack the driving power of the Monad. The detrimental qualitites of Number Six belong to these people too. They may set too much store on knowledge for knowledge's sake, may be lethargic and dreamy, dabble in too many fields without making a success of any, and drift with the tide. These people need to learn self discipline in work and concentration, and to value the natural gifts they have been given as a way of benefiting both themselves and the world at large. The Number Nine rules dark brown or dark blue touched with streaks of white. This colour aids concentration and hope.

CHAPTER 5

Your Love and Marriage Number: The Kabbala

We have dealt with the primary numbers: now, in addition, we will deal with those numbers associated with the Kabbala, the collection of traditional knowledge of the Ancient Hebrews. The Hebrew alphabet contains twenty-two letters. Since our alphabet has twenty-six letters, there will be some letters with the same number, and since some single letters in the Greek alphabet can only be represented by two of ours, there are four pairs of letters which have a special value. These are:

$$
\begin{array}{ccccc}
TH & = & Theta & = & 8 \\
PH & = & Phi & = & 3 \\
CH & = & Chi & = & 4 \\
PS & = & Psi & = & 5 \\
\end{array}
$$

So, when we come across these combinations in a name, for example 'Kathleen' or 'Theodore', they must be valued as a single number, not as two separate letters.

A	=	1	J	=	1	S	=	1
B	=	2	K	=	2	T	=	2
C	=	3	L	=	3	U	=	3
D	=	4	M	=	4	V	=	4
E	=	5	N	=	5	W	=	5
F	=	6	O	=	6	X	=	6
G	=	7	P	=	7	Y	=	7
H	=	8	Q	=	8	Z	=	8
I	=	9	R	=	9			

Numbers are traditionally linked with the planets and each has a Zodiacal ruler. They are as follows:

One:	Sun Positive
Two:	Moon Negative
Three:	Jupiter
Four:	Sun Negative
Five:	Mercury
Six:	Venus
Seven:	Moon Positive
Eight:	Saturn
Nine:	Mars
Ten:	Uranus

How We Find the Marriage Number

If we know the potentialities of the love and marriage numbers we can see if the vibrations are harmonious with a prospective marriage partner.

First we must take all the first names and the surname of both parties, and the correct birth date of each party. Then we analyse them, using both systems. The unit or 'primary' system, applied to the birth date, gives us the harmonious or conflicting relationships between our numbers and theirs, and the Kabbala system, applied to the full name, taking into account also the Zodiacal influence, gives an interpretation of marital possibilities. When there is more than one first name these names are totalled invidually, then added together, with the surname.

First we will take the birthday, 20 May 1929. The way we add it together would astonish most mathematicians, so be careful. Adding across you start simply enough, taking '20' from the date and '5' from the month of May — the fifth month of the year. But when you add them, the answer is not '25' but '7'. Why? Because we *literally* add from left to right. So what we say is '2 plus 0 plus 5 equals 7'; then we go on to the year, '1929', '1 plus 9 plus 2 plus 9 equals 21'. Add that to the 7 you already have and the answer is '28'.

But that is not the final answer. We have to take another step and add together the 2 and the 8 of 28. The answer, of course, is 10: another double figure. But since 1 plus 0 equals 1, our *final* answer is '1'. So that

person is ruled by the Character of Primary number '1'.
Here is the calculation once again:

(1) 20 May 1929
(2) 20 + 5 + 1929

or (3) 2 + 0 + 5 + 1 + 9 + 2 + 9 = 28
(4) 2 + 8   = 10
(5) 1 + 0   = 1

Then we go on to evaluate the person's name, using the Kabbala system. Let us say her name is Alison Rosalie Brainwood. When we write it down, with the Kabbala number beneath each letter, it looks like this:

A   L   I   S   O   N
1 + 3 + 9 + 1 + 6 + 5
R   O   S   A   L   I   E
9 + 6 + 1 + 1 + 3 + 9 + 5
B   R   A   I   N   W   O   O   D
2 + 9 + 1 + 9 + 5 + 5 + 6 + 6 + 4

Now let's start adding up each name from left to right once more:

A   L   I   S   O   N
1 + 3 + 9 + 1 + 6 + 5 = 25
R   O   S   A   L   I   E
9 + 6 + 1 + 1 + 3 + 9 + 5 = 34
B   R   A   I   N   W   O   O   D
2 + 9 + 1 + 9 + 5 + 5 + 6 + 6 + 4 = 47

Carry on as you did before:

2 + 5 = 7   3 + 4 = 7   4 + 7 = 11
                                  1 + 1 = 2

So 'Alison' is 7, 'Rosalie' is 7 and 'Brainwood' is 2. And the last part of your sum is:

$$7 + 7 + 2 = 16$$
$$1 + 6 = 7$$

So the the girl's marriage number is 7. Now, what about the man she is interested in?

E   D   W   A   R   D
5 + 4 + 5 + 1 + 9 + 4 = 28
B   R   I   A   N
2 + 9 + 9 + 1 + 5 = 26
M   c   M   A   H   O   N
4 + 3 + 4 + 1 + 8 + 6 + 5 = 31

$$2 + 8 = 10; \ 1 + 0 = 1 \qquad 2 + 6 = 8 \qquad 3 + 1 = 4$$

$1 + 8 + 4 = 13$, and $1 + 3 = 4$, so his marriage number is 4. As for his character number, we know he was born on 17 November 1925, the eleventh month of the year. So the sum looks like this:

$$1 + 7 + 1 + 1 + 1 + 9 + 2 + 5 = 27$$
$$2 + 7 = 9$$

His marriage number is 4 and his character number is 9.

Now we look up the tables to see whether these two people would have a happy marriage. Remember, the primary or character numbers are listed in the previous chapter and here are the Love and Marriage Numbers, followed by the Table of Harmonies which tells you which of the marriage numbers respond best to one another.

CHAPTER 6

Love and Marriage Numbers

Number One
This number is the number of romance, and yet the attraction must have an intellectual basis. Because this number also stands for variety, it will be difficult to bring about a lasting attachment, for there is the tendency to have two irons in the fire at the same time. Also, the accent on intellectuality will often preclude the warmth of passion, for which you will look in vain. Marriages could be brought about suddenly, and meetings could take place while travelling away from home, or in a place of learning. This number would always have to exercise caution in married life, for there could be the danger of extramarital affairs through boredom or loss of mental freedom.

Number Two
This number is discriminating in its choice of a marriage partner, mainly because the love of comfort and stability is foremost. Suggestion can play an important part in the life of this subject, and you would be wise to check undue criticism or interference on the part of in-laws or friends. There can also be secret friendships made of a purely platonic nature, which must be handled adroitly to prevent marital trouble. You will demand a person with a good mind, but one who is eminently practical and able to amply provide the financial security you desire.

Number Three
You have the misfortune to meet ideal partners too late, when they are married, and if not careful could be making one side of a triangle instead of keeping your eye out for another suitable marriage partner who is free. You are idealistic and long for partnership in marriage,

but your spirit of sacrifice can be abused sadly by those in whom you put your trust. Possibly there will have been one or more 'near misses' for you, for you have the protection which prevents you from tying the knot with a person of unsuitable temperament or inferior character. If you let your intuition take over, your choice will be unerring, for you understand people's motives very well, and will usually pick someone whose interests match with yours, making for a very companionable life.

Number Four
You are attracted strongly to marriage by your emotional and affectionate nature, but your discretion at times is poor, and your choice can lead you into difficulties. You will find the way made more difficult for you by the envy and spite of others, and also by your own tendency to take others too literally. You will be attracted by an active and dominant partner, and yet there is a part of your character that hates being hurried, dominated or bossed around, so that domestic friction can occur at times. Your partner should be interested in occult matters, and should be able to hold your interest by his intellectual superiority.

Number Five
These people marry for life, because they are sincere and honourable, but curiously there is often a history of broken romances before marriage through the lack of sincerity of the other party. If hurt in this way you will find it hard to pick up the reins again, and if widowed after a happy marriage, it is seldom that these people marry again. Religion and philosophy play a large part in your life, and although the sex urge is strong, there is a feeling of restraint that prevents you from indulgence in sex before marriage. Companionship is vital to you and because the courtship is usually conducted in a commonsense way that stresses shared activities, the marriage will be happy and loving.

Number Six
Usually late blossomers, these people, although ardent underneath, are shy and unable to express themselves. However they have, through inner impatience, periods of rash behaviour during which, if they are not careful, they can form alliances of a very unsatisfactory nature

which if carried through to marriage can bring untold unhappiness. A weak number, denoting vacillation and variety, you must guard against the desire for new companionship which could disturb the married state, particularly if you are away from the marriage partner. If your marriage takes place after the age of thirty-three, then there will be more hope for its success and stability.

Number Seven

This number is often designated as a flirt. This is not so, although these people should not marry in their teens before their character and taste are moulded. They are so active both mentally and physically that their existence is varied and they tend to meet far more people than the other numbers with the exception of five. They often have more than one marriage in life, and numerous affairs, but once they are married, they do not seek diversion. Often in their life there will be many partings from loved ones and friends, and even deaths around them from their earliest years. They are also usually burdened with responsibility from an early age.

Number Eight

This number brings travel, change and variety. You may have more than one marriage, and possibly more than one divorce, through your innate restlessness and love of change. Often also your marital life is bound up with your spouse's business life or you could work together in a family business. Obstacles and delays are a feature of your earlier years, and the happiest marriage for you would be a marriage with an older person and when you yourself are over thirty.

Number Nine

Marriage is your gateway to the fulfilled life, and to this end you bend all your thoughts, hopes and wishes from an early age. You tend to be attracted when young to people much older than yourself, and this in certain cases could bring unhappiness, particularly later in life when you will in turn be attracted to younger people. Care should be taken to make sure that your aims and activities together with the motivation are commensurate with your partner's, as failure of one to keep up with the other in any of these aspects could cause much frustration and unhappiness.

And now for the Table of Harmonies in which you can see whether your own and your partner's numbers can make together a successful recipe for marriage.

Similar numbers will give great accord and harmony, albeit a little too peaceful. If a number vibrates to another it means the attraction is strong and mutual. If the number attracts another number, this shows that the two people are compatible. When the number disagrees or opposes another, then there would have to be a large measure of diplomacy used constantly to prevent this union from foundering. In the case of a number which is merely passive to another, there are no outstanding influences connected with this union, either fortunate or unfortunate.

Table of Harmonies

Number One: This number vibrates to 9.
Attracts 4 & 8.
Is opposed to 6 & 7.
Is passive to 2, 3 & 5.

Number Two: This number vibrates to 8.
Attracts 7, 9 and 1.
Is opposed to 5.
Is passive to 3, 4 & 6.

Number Three: This number vibrates to 7.
Attracts 5, 6 and 9.
Is opposed to 4 & 8.
Is passive to 1 & 2.

Number Four: This number vibrates to 6.
Attracts 1 & 8.
Is opposed to 5.
Is passive to 2, 7, 9 & 3.

Number Five: This number vibrates to another 5.
Attracts 3, 9 & 2.
Is opposed to 4.
Is passive to 1, 6, 7 & 8.

Number Six: This number vibrates to 4 & 2.
Attracts 3 & 9.
Is mildly opposed to 1 & 8; deeply opposed to 5..
Is passive to 7.

Number Seven: This number vibrates to 3 & 5.
Attracts 2 & 6.
Is opposed to 1 & 9.
Is passive to 4 & 8.

Number Eight: This number vibrates to 2 & 5.
Attracts 1 & 4.
Is opposed to 3 & 6.
Is passive to 7 & 9.

Number Nine: This number vibrates to 1.
Attracts 2, 3 & 6.
Is opposed to 7.
Is passive to 4, 5 & 8.

CHAPTER 7

Your House Numbers

The number of your house can tell you what vibrations abound there, and taking the table of positive and negative attractions, you can compare your own number with that of your abode and this will enable you to see whether your surroundings are harmonious or working against you in a subtle way.

Add together all the numbers of your house, and if it has a name add the letters too, and total these. If you live in a flat then you add the number of your apartment to the street number too. Temporary abodes, such as boarding houses, hotels and motels are not conducive to vibrations, for there are too many people passing through their portals. If you find that the number is definitely incompatible, and particularly if your house has a name, then I would suggest you rename it so that the vibrations are favourable.

Number One
Impeccable in taste and just a little bit self righteous and smug in atmosphere, this home has an aura of domineering females, career people, and lot of white woodwork and furniture. It would be a good house in winter, but demanding quite a lot of heating, and could be stark in its early years, but mellows in later years through plenty of greenery and a lessening of discipline. There will always be organization, discipline and a firm sense of right and wrong in this house, but perhaps too much intolerance for the weaker or less wealthy person.

Number Two
This house is generally a little run down, but in a pleasant, comfortable way. There are lots of people in and out of this house. It should be

a sociable dwelling. Its outside appearance is usually at variance with its interior, as if the people living there are more concerned with what the neighbours think than they ought to be. The smaller details are meticulously cared for whereas the really important things such as drains, roofs and heating can sometimes be neglected. People in the public eye often live in a Number Two dwelling, particularly those connected with words, either spoken or written. There will be a danger of severe nervous breakdowns for the occupants of this number house. Autumn is the most pleasant season, and the house will attract both the young and the young at heart. The occupants of this house could, through their instability and temptation, have one or more love affairs which could prove harmful to their more stable associations.

Number Three
This house could have a lot of unfinished projects within its walls, both of renovation and innovation. The occupants are original and enterprising, interested in new inventions, everything pertaining to the mind, but sometimes there is too little cohesion and concentration on the task in hand. The occupants could marry early, then divorce and later make a more suitable union. Summer is the season for this dwelling because the occupants of a Number Three house like to be out and about, exploring, fishing, boating, swimming, walking and attending the exhibitions of art that they love. The home itself will be originally and artistically furnished, and even if there is little ready money available the result will look elegant and expensive.

Number Four
This dwelling will have endured lots of changes, and repairs that have been hastily effected. It is the home of the do it yourself decorator, carpenter and upholsterer. New gadgets will abound, but there will be carelessness with the household goods, even flooding and electrical faults causing damage and yet the atmosphere is happy go lucky and welcoming. There will be little financial security, not through any lack of ability, but through lack of confidence and drive, which would have to be remedied before the true worth of the occupant will be realized. There is a marked preference for status and prestige, rather than for money, dignity and worth. Spring is the season for this house, as there

will be a renewal of energy and ambition which should be utilized before it is too late.

Number Five

This house is often the dwelling of the famous, or those in the public eye. It is solidly built, and usually sports some flowers or shrubs, even if they are in pots. It is the natural dwelling-place of the cosmopolitan, and should be varied in its furnishings and even architecture, or original and made over from some other type of dwelling. Spacious, or with a sense of space, a little lonely because of the occupants' selectivity in choosing friends, or the necessities of his profession which demand privacy, nevertheless it has an aura of tolerance, wit and kindliness. Blues and greens should be featured in this house, and there should be plenty of window space and fresh air to prevent respiratory troubles. This house blossoms in April and May.

Number Six

A house of harmony, usually the dwelling of the artistically gifted, it is full of colour, balance, original ideas, cleverly made over furniture, old objects, particularly brass and silver. The inhabitants can either be striving for wordly acclaim, and so breeding disruption and frustration, or be living for the moment and so letting their opportunities pass them by. There is never a lack of food or material goods in this house. In fact, often there will be two sets of things, two identical pieces of furniture which turn up in strange ways, but there will be a definite lack of money, as extravagance in purchasing beautiful objects, books or records is the failing of these Number Six occupants. The house can often be draughty and kidney chills must be avoided, but apart from that winter is the season of renewal for this house.

Number Seven

This house has a sense of unreality or impermanence through being occupied by a series of tenants. The Number Seven house has an aura of make believe. Many of its occupants are hiding behind a facade, often deluding themselves that they are more important or wealthier than they really are. The house has a very attractive exterior at first glance, and the illusion of wealth is carried inside, but when one looks closely one sees the shabbiness, the artifice and often the despoliation of a beautiful architectural feature or a genuine historic building which has been prettied up and lost its character. The occupants have to guard against overspending and illogical thinking. The house will bloom in early spring which holds the promise of a more realistic beginning again, if the people there will take stock.

Number Eight

Number Eight houses have an air of permanence, of endurance, stolidity and unostentatious wealth. The owners of a Number Eight house will possibly own other property, and may have owned land around the house which they have subdivided and sold. There is an aura around this house, as if the people are used to being obeyed and consider there is only one point of view, theirs! A house where changes take place slowly, and renovations or additions are done painstakingly and in keeping with the other parts of the dwelling. There could be troubles over the physical side of love in this Number Eight house, and many occupants could be living with their partners in a state of unarmed warfare, or may have called a truce so that their relationship is polite, cold and sterile. Manipulation of finances can lead this number to extremes, either of great wealth or of sudden total loss. There could be trouble with damp coursing and drains, and the house will be expensive to heat in winter. The middle of each of the four seasons is the best time for this house.

Number Nine

The occupants of this house will have many plans, too many for practicality. They should go to their bank manager and talk out their long range plans with him, otherwise their finances will get into a muddle. They have a lot of trials and tribulations in their early days through in-laws and children, incurring expense and suffering illness, so that they should not be too ambitious when starting their home and family, but wait until they have reached middle age and their children are off their hands, before modernizing their premises or taking that long trip. Then they will be more fortunate, for the latter half of their lives will be much happier. Builders and painters could live happily at this number. They will have much love and affection from their family as they grow older, and will be found in all corners of the world, visiting their offspring or touring the places they so badly wanted to see when young and tied down by responsibility. July and August are the good months for this house, and it has only one drawback: it could be near a noisy road or airfield, causing its inhabitants to suffer from insomnia.

CHAPTER 8

Love is on the Cards

Although the Tarot cards are mainly used to foretell future spiritual and material progress through life and give a wide view of events, it is possible to answer questions concerning romance by using only those cards which pertain to romance which are the fourteen cards of the suit of Cups, and the twenty-two 'picture cards', known as the Major Arcana plus the other court cards.

There are seventy-eight cards in the Tarot pack, twenty-two Major Arcana and fifty-six Minor Arcana, split into four suits, Cups, Coins, Swords and Staves, each containing fourteen cards. There is one extra court card, the Knave, which was dropped when our modern pack of playing cards was devised for the game of Picquet in the sixteenth century.

The suit of Cups represents all matters to do with pleasure, domestic affairs and love in every aspect. The Swords suit represents spiritual struggle and growth, great effort of will, opposition, suffering and sorrow. The Coins suit represents all matters pertaining to money, luxury, inheritance, gifts, miserliness, greed, selfishness and materialism. The Staves relate to artistic talent, triumph after sustained effort, expansion in a creative and spiritual sense, solid balance and lasting security.

Because of the limited number of cards used it is necessary to remember the subsidiary meanings of each card, for no card has one meaning only, nor can it stand in isolation, its meaning being heightened, or modified by the cards around it. The art of reading, which can only come with practice, is of learning to link them together to give a sensible interpretation.

The Tarot tradition is for one person desiring a reading, to ask a question of the cards, and, according to belief, the less selfish the query, the more satisfactory the answer will be, for the Tarot's main accent is on the spiritual aspect of life.

The person reading is called the Reader, the person desiring a reading, the Enquirer. The court cards, apart from having some separate meanings, represent people of differing ages and colourings. As there are twelve male court cards in the Tarot pack and only four female cards, we cannot set an age for the Queens, but the male ages are:

The Knave	Infancy to eighteen (these can sometimes be female)
The Knight	Eighteen to thirty-five
The King	Thirty-five onwards

Sometimes, but not often, an over-serious young man can turn up in the cards as a King, and a 'Peter Pan' type of older man can be portrayed as a Knight.

Three Knights, (side by side) mean police, four knights appearing side by side, can mean the armed forces or simply an all-male gathering, two Kings or two Knights denote legal or medical men, three Kings usually denote a change of direction in life and a gathering of three or more Knaves, means either workmen about the house, a rowdy party, or activities relating to adolescents of either sex.

Before laying the cards out in a position called a Spread, the Reader must choose a card, appropriate in age and colouring to represent the Enquirer. He must note the skin, eyes and hair in that order; the determining factor being the tone of the skin.

Swords stand for the Latin colouring, dark olive skin, black or brown eyes and black or brown hair. Staves stand for light olive skin, brown hazel or green eyes, and dark brown to light brown hair. Cups stand for fair or rosy complexioned people, blue, grey, hazel, sometimes green eyes and Coins have the same eyes with blond, white, golden or red hair. If a person's hair had whitened with age, they will drop one tone, so that with the exception of Coins, the fairest, Swords become Staves, Staves become Cups and Cups Pentacles. These distinctions must be taken into account when reading the Queens and Kings, particularly if there are other indications to suggest age, such as power, authority or illness.

The Meanings of the Cups Suit
The Court Cards

The King of Cups — The Husband Card
Fair complexioned, light-eyed, brown haired man over thirty-five years of age. Denotes the husband. If with another King, a professional man.

The Queen of Cups — The Wife Card (also Happy Marriage Card)
Fair complexioned, light eyed, brown haired woman. Denotes the wife. It also means a happy marriage, or that the Enquirer is a good mixer.

The Knight of Cups — The Proposal Card
Fair complexioned, light eyed, brown haired man from eighteen to thirty-five, usually a bachelor. This card also can mean a proposal or invitation.

The Knave of Cups — The News Bringer, Child of Either Sex
Fair complexioned youth or child of either sex, it also means the birth of a child, or the start of something new, and also new methods in business.

The Number Cards

Ten of Cups — The Fame and Prestige Card
This stands for public esteem, even fame, the respect of friends — work done for the public which brings happiness and acclaim. It also denotes a happy secure domestic circle, the house or the home town of the Enquirer.

Nine of Cups — The Wish Card
Fame and success — emotional security — dreams come true — good luck — good health — sudden unexpected gifts or gain through loved ones. If placed near negative cards ('badly placed') it cannot lose its strength, but benefits will be delayed through the Enquirers own negativity or wrong thinking.

The Eight of Cups — New and Happy Horizons
This card denotes new experiences — new friends, new work and

interests, saying goodbye to the unhappy past. With other love cards, (The Lovers, the two the nine or the Ace), it can mean a marriage and happy removal. It can mean rewards for past actions, a small journey, a pleasure trip or happiness at the end of a holiday journey, and sometimes a removal of home. If badly placed, it means the Enquirer must make a positive decision to end a frustrating situation.

The Seven of Cups — The Multi-Talented Dreamer
A sudden stroke of luck will benefit artistic endeavour, or something recently commenced. Mental activity and creative talent are denoted here, but the correct choice will have to be made in order to succeed. If negatively placed, it denotes an unrealistic dreamer — a Jack of All Trades — with little grasp of practical details. It can also mean that a wrong choice will be made through self-deception or failure because of the inability to make a choice.

The Six of Cups — Our End is in Our Beginnings
The Family or Past card — starting a family — past associations, past activities which have relevance in the present. It can bring old friends back into the Enquirers life — or that he or she is looking back on something for the last time — it is severing past ties — or a dream from the past will now be realised. If badly placed, it means that the Enquirer tends to live too much in the past — or could be dominated by the family and is frightened to break away.

The Five of Cups — The Cross Roads of Life
The card of inheritance — of something gained, but always with the thought of something regretted or lost — remembrance after a separation from a lover or friend who has gone away or died. The cross roads — a decision to make — new alternatives to be explored. If badly placed, it means that love has been lost. It can also denote that the Enquirer suffers from a lack of confidence, and is hesitant or indecisive.

The Four of Cups — The Divine Discontent Card
The state of dissatisfaction which is always the forerunner of change and improvement. It can sometimes, if coming near a court card, mean that outside interference will change the course of a love affair. If badly

placed, it can denote that the Enquirer's own discontented attitude to life will mar a future change of circumstances and that he or she does not possess the gift of gratitude.

The Three of Cups — Hopes Fulfilled

A happy card, denoting the joyous conclusion of an emotional matter as well as meaning fame and success in any artistic endeavour in which the emotions are called into play such as writing, singing, acting. It can also mean a happy nuptial celebration if near the marriage cards (The Lovers of the Major Arcana, The Ace, The Two or the Nine.)

The Two of Cups — Engagement Card

The card of loving unions, alliances, the signing of papers or contracts. It means friendship, companionship, as well as reconciliation after a parting. It is the homosexual card, and if shown with the Moon has the connotation of hidden or latent aberration. If badly placed, can mean difficulties in partnership will arise.

The Ace of Cups — The Marriage Card

The marriage card, in this case, it, like all the other aces, stands for new beginnings in the emotional sense. It also means creative talent which brings warmth, pleasure and talent to others in a new undertaking and can denote spiritual inspiration, or a loving, giving nature.

The Major Arcana

The Magician — Number One — The Commencement Card

This card carries the connotation of quick action, mental activity, communication, skill with words, as well as occult power. It stands for initiative, willpower, self-awareness, the ability to translate thought into action taking risks which result in triumph, learning, new skills, new facts, new careers and the guidance of occult forces. When negatively aspected, that is, when surrounded by cards which have negative meanings, it denotes guile or trickery, uncertainty or using and abusing occult power for selfish ends.

The High Priestess — Number Two — Healing and Spiritual Awareness

This card stands for Divination — Mysticism, Esoteric knowledge, a thirst for learning, creative talent, often denoting the healer, the teacher, doctor, nurse, and hospitals as well as qualifications gained by study. It also means a deep religious conviction, safety by spiritual guidance, intuition or psychic power, as well as cultural activities such as deal with the written word, e.g. publishing, writing drama, television drama, and those that deal with the visually beautiful, such as art, fabrics, antiques. When next to (a) The Emperor or (b) Justice, can mean (a) a diplomat or (b) a high court judge.

The Empress — Number Three — The Horn of Plenty
The Empress represents abundance and fertility both in the agricultural and artistic sense, motherhood, a flowering of emotional and intuitive feeling, domestic harmony, stability, increased prosperity, also artistic abundance, good health, a benefactor, a generous and happy spirit, a force for good and sometimes a wealthy marriage.

The Emperor — Number Four — Majesty and Might
This card, as opposed to the intuition of the Empress, stands for logic, the triumph of intelligence over passion, energy, temporal power, knowledge through experience, stability, leadership, wealth, great influence and governing the masses. It can denote a government or government official, a Multi National Business and the country of Great Britain. When next to Justice can mean a politician.

The Heirophant — Number Five — The Public View
One meaning of this card is a preference for ritualistic religion or the desire for society's approval. It can also mean secrets revealed, as well as denoting a scientific or religious person, and a late vocation being realized. It is the inspirational card of the performing arts, particularly of music but can also denote the university lecturer, or any occupation which serves the public.

The Lovers — Number Six — Emotional Choice
The meaning of this card is always underlaid by a choice or the freedom of choice. It denotes the emotions — a love affair — a marriage, also idealistic friendship. It can denote a moral choice causing suffering

and, sometimes, means a flash of insight which resolves a moral problem.

The Chariot — Number Seven — Well-Earned Triumph
The card that means triumph through personal sustained effort and victory through control, always such a connotation of arrival, it is never inherited success. It can mean greatness particularly in creative work. It also means triumph over difficulties, over ill-health, and over poverty bringing wealth and honour. It also denotes the routing of enemies — unexpected news by word of mouth, or sometimes travel in luxurious conditions. Only when coupled with The Tower or Death could this card be considered negative, when it could be read as the sudden collapse of a plan.

Strength — Number Eight — Right is Might
This card is the strongest in the Tarot and influences all others so that any negative influence is lessened. This is the spiritual overcoming the material. It denotes integrity, and means that the Enquirers own moral strength will overcome all difficulties. It denotes events overcome by willpower, self-discipline, endurance, tolerance, overcoming prejudice, and the mastery of life. On a more mundane level a wonderful opportunity will arise which, if the Enquirer has the courage to grasp, will lead to great happiness.

The Hermit — Number Nine — Divine Guidance By The Inner Light
This card is the card of slow careful progress leading to attainment. It is sometimes a warning that prudence and careful planning is needed or that the inner voice should be listened to more often and can also mean the slowing down of events. It can simply mean that the Enquirer will be given advice, or guidance, sometimes legal which will benefit him or her, or it can mean a prospective long journey or the yearning for travel. If negatively placed, it can denote excess timidity is retarding events or that the Enquirer has refused to face adult responsibilities. It can also mean a delay caused by his or her procrastination.

The Wheel of Fortune — Number Ten — Karmic Reward and Luck
The Wheel of Fortune means sudden gain, usually unexpected, happiness, success and material prosperity. It has the connotation of

something deserved or earned spiritually. On a deeper level, it can also mean the gaining of wisdom and balance, and is seldom ever unfortunate unless very badly placed, with the The Devil or The Moon, then it can mean that great benefits are being delayed by the Enquirers own negative attitude to life.

Justice — Number Eleven — 'As Ye Sow So Shall Ye Reap'
This is Spiritual Justice or Karma and can also mean that the Enquirer will gain great prestige or reknown. It also means that he or she has a well-balanced outlook and, like the Hermit can denote a trial of conscience as well as meaning an actual trial, rehabilitation, justice and honesty, favourable outcome of a legal or educational matter. It also denotes the Vindication of the moral integrity of the Enquirer. When with the Hermit could denote a high legal position and if accompanied by the Emperor — a leader of government.

The Hanged Man — Number Twelve — Spiritual Sacrifice Brings Inward Peace
Not always a happy card, it means renunciation of both actual and spiritual, self-sacrifice and abandonment. It can mean a difficult moral decision results in inward peace, and also denotes occult or prophetic power, intuition, wisdom from above. On a mundane level it can mean suspended decision, a pause or a period of calm or a delay in ones affairs.

Death — Number Thirteen — The Transformation Card
This card originally stood for the death of Kings and Princes, and although it can mean death, it carries today more the meaning of transformation, change, or the blessed destruction which heralds a new life. It can also mean the beginning of new creative activity.

Temperance — Number Fourteen — The Card of Combination
This card stands for adaptation to circumstances, co-ordination, good management of warring elements in a situation, the successful combination of new elements with the old, or simply a position of management. It is a happy card, bringing fruitfulness, new life, vitality, moderation and sometimes can mean a wealthy and successful marriage. It can denote a well-balanced personality.

The Devil —Number Fifteen — Irrevocable Event

This card, although powerful, is not always unfortunate, depending upon the integrity and spirituality of the Enquirer. If the Strength card is present, it can simply mean that a sudden unexpected irrevocable event will alter future plans. However, it stands for the domination of the material over the spiritual, and can bring force, violence, revolution, catastrophe, illness and an almost overwhelming temptation which will be difficult to resist. Not surprisingly, it also means the gratification of the lusts of the body at the expense of the higher nature.

The Tower — Number Sixteen — The Phoenix Rising

This card always has the meaning of suddenness. Apart from denoting the selfish ambitions being brought to dust, sudden disruption of a blow of fate there is a Karmic meaning of the end of Life's lessons and the attainment that leads to a higher existence. On a more mundane level it can simply mean sudden unexpected change which could alter the pattern of life, or overthrow present plans. It always carries the connotation of something better, once the dust has settled, arising out of the chaos, even when surrounded by other negative cards.

The Star — Number Seventeen — Rebirth of Joy, Love and Hope

This card is never negative. It means unselfish help given, hope, optimism, renewed effort after disappointments, the courage to try again (particularly after a broken marriage), new inspiration for the artist, and renewed health for the invalid. It can mean if placed with a negative card, that the Enquirer tends to give into pessimism or intolerance through fear.

The Moon — Number Eighteen — The Subconscious World of Dreams

The card of illusion, deception, mental illness, things hidden below the surface, a cancer hidden from view, and sometimes the actual illness, as well as denoting the sea and the East. Although it is often a negative card, there is also the meaning of creativity, and artistic imagination. But it can mean a crisis of faith which only the Enquirer can deal with, and misfortune or an accident to loved ones. It can be a warning that commonsense must triumph over a too active imagination.

The Sun — Number Nineteen — Triumph and Success
This card is always happy, and like the Chariot means triumph after effort, but as a culmination whereas the Chariot always has the connotation of speed. It means the end of study, freedom from restriction, and often means fame and rewards or the realization of ambitions. One of its nicest meanings is the gift of gratitude for the blessings of life. It is unalterable and modifies any surrounding negative cards.

The Judgement — Number Twenty — New Life-Rebirth
Although rather alarming at first view, this is always a good card, meaning renewal, rebirth or the mental and spiritual awakening that precedes happiness and fulfilment. It is a highly spiritual card, meaning regrowth and progress, the shaking out of a rut, or on a more mundane level, a beneficial change of work. If with Justice or the Hermit and The Lovers it can mean a divorce. But if with the The Devil or The Moon, it could mean the change or benefit may or may not be lasting, according to the moral strength of the Enquirer.

The World — Number Twenty One — Hearts Desire Card
This is the card of the perfectionist, or the person who is learning his lessons and is receiving his reward. It is the 'wish' card of the Major Arcana, bringing the triumph of the individual, love, joy and happiness and completion. It can also denote long water journeys. If negatively placed, it means the Enquirer is unable to change his or her life patterns, because of his attachment to certain conditions and places, but these will be overcome in time.

The Fool — Number 0 — The Divine Questing Child
This card means spiritual guidance through life — a blithe spirit who does not rely on material sources for its nourishment or strength, or a vital choice to be made. It also denotes travel or movement, sometimes meaning a purely spiritual journey. If placed badly can also mean extravagance, eccentricity, rebellion against the conventional authority and highlights the irresponsible element in human nature. Sometimes, although it denotes the Enquirer is highly spiritual it can also mean that he is aimlessly wandering through life, without a goal.

The Mystic Star Spread

Before we deal with the procedure of reading the Tarot and using the Spread called the Mystic Star, there are a few points to be kept in mind.

Because we are using a limited number of cards, and some of the court cards have important subsidiary meanings apart from representing people, such as:

The Queen of Cups standing for the wife, or a happy marriage;
The King of Cups standing for the husband;
The King of Swords standing for a government official, or foreigner;
The Knight of Staves standing for emigration or a long journey;
The Queen of Swords standing either for a widow or a foreign country;
The Knight of Cups standing for a proposal;
The Knave of Swords standing for being watched or a deliberate thinker;
The Queen of Coins standing for mother.

as well as others given, it will be necessary to work around them. To do this, we will have to use either the suit of Coins or Staves, (which have fewer auxiliary meanings) for the Enquirer, substituting the Knight of Coins for the Knight of Staves, but remembering always that most of the court cards do have meanings other than simply representing men or women.

Firstly choose the appropriate card for the Enquirer, place it on the table and shuffle the pack before handing it to the Enquirer and asking him to make three random cuts and then place the three piles face down in front of him, with the left hand — the hand of the Devil as it was once called, or in modern pyschological terms, the hand of the deep Unconscious which motivates our conscious behaviour. Turn the three packs upwards, and read the three cards individually and in combination. These are thought to give a general indication of whether the reading will be fortunate or otherwise. (For the purpose of the reading illustrated here we have chosen a female Enquirer — The Queen of Staves.)

Then lay out eight cards, keeping the Enquirer's card in the middle, in an anti-clockwise direction, as in the illustration. Each point of the star deals with a different aspect of the reading.

Now hand back the pack to the Enquirer and ask him first to shuffle

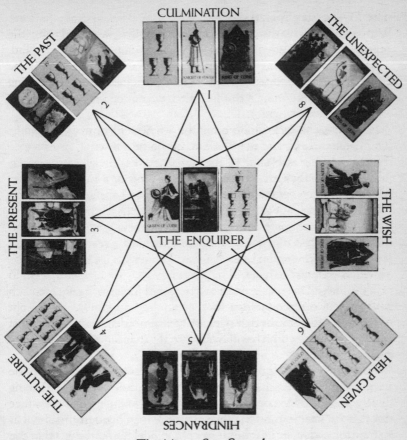

The Mystic Star Spread

the pack again and then to lay two cards, in the same order on top of the first eight cards.

There will now be eight piles of three cards, and the Enquirer's card in the middle. Now, pick two cards yourself, at random from the pack and cover the Enquirer's card, so that there will be twenty-seven cards laid out in the Spread.

Now you, the Reader, turns over the three cards in the first pile, starting with Pile number two, 'The Past', and read each pile, linking them together to make a story. The two cards covering the Enquirer's card, can be very important, as they can weaken or strengthen the Wish or the Culmination, and can also act as a check or a timely warning as to the wisdom of future actions of the Enquirer.

In the illustration given, the three cards in the Past pack; the Moon, the Four of Cups and Judgement could denote that the Enquirer has endured a separation or a divorce after deception and is not happy with the present situation.

In the Present Pack, there could be a new start in work, possibly under government, and the Enquirer could be a teacher, or nurse or work with a big publisher in the future.

In the Future Pack, the Enquirer could be meeting a lover in a foreign country, perhaps on holiday, or through a widow friend or relative.

In the Hindrances Pack, it is possible to read these cards as meaning there will be some upheaval and sacrifice in business, which will interfere with the progress of the romance, or it could be read over sudden serious issue coming up over religion. Which would entail sacrifice on either partners part.

In the Help Given Pack, there will be an old friend or family member who will effect a reconciliation.

The Wish Pack shows that strength will be needed, and the Enquirer has moral strength, which will overcome all obstacles and that a happy marriage with a foreigner will be the result.

The Unexpected Pack, certainly is unexpected, having the Tower amongst the three cards, as well as Death. It could mean simply that there will be a sudden death of a man, or a nicer interpretation is that through the meeting and the love affair the man in question's life will be transformed from a bachelor gay to a model husband, and that the man could be a professional man or wearing a uniform.

The Culmination Pack is happy and all that the Enquirer would ask for. The rejoicing of the Three of Cups, is accompanied by the long journey card, and the King of Pentacles, so now we have a picture of the man she will meet, and know that she will accompany him overseas to Australia, America, Canada or Africa, where he obviously comes from.

Now, the two cards which cover the Enquirer are the Hermit and the Five of Cups which very clearly show indecision, perhaps the need for caution, but more strongly the suggestion that the Enquirer tends to lack confidence in a decision and instead of asking other people must listen to her own intuition or she will lose her chance of happiness.

CHAPTER 9

Lovers in Dreamland: The Meaning of Dreams

Some dreams bring us prophetic glimpses of the future, some are strong warnings. Some are caused organically, stemming from an alteration from the blood flow to the brain, some are artificially produced through self-suggestion. And some are inspirational, often supplying us from our subsconscious mind with the answer to a problem we have been wrestling with on a conscious level. The general belief that dreams go by opposites could be said to be largely correct and it has its explanation in the sleeping mind. This sometimes loses the power to make contrasts. There occurs then a unification of opposites where we are unable to draw distinctions between black and white, backwards and forward, joy and sorrow. The ancients in a general sense recognized this and compiled a history of significant dreams and the events following, which in turn led to a detailed collection of interpreted meanings, these in turn were collected and edited by Artemidorus, a Roman seer, who gathered material from many races and sources and compiled a massive work, 'The Five Books of the Interpretations of Dreams and Visions', which has come down to us as being valid for those dreams which are purely prophetic.

Many of the dreams were connected with love, courtship and children and from there I have carefully selected those most pertinent to the lover today. But remember, the interpretation is of necessity, as it pertains to the tricky subconscious, and can be modified or altered slightly according to the subject's own inner feelings or intuitions.

Many dreams appear to have been overlooked because there has been no ancient authority or modern psychologist to give them significance, but the reader himself may be quite able to find the key, particularly if the dream occurs before a certain chain of events in his life. It may be then that he will realise his subconscious is either warning him or giving him a prophetic vision.

Dream Subjects

Abandonment: To abandon someone denotes a renewal of an old friendship; if you are abandoned, there will be a quarrel with an old friend.

Accident: To be involved in a road accident or see one means you are placing your trust in one who will betray you.

Adder: To be bitten by a snake or adder betokens treachery coming from a false friend. To see yourself killing an adder means an end to an undesirable friendship.

Altar: An unhappy dream if you are standing before it — signifying losses and illness. However, if you are a decorating an altar, a happy love affair is in the offing.

Angels: For those in love, a happy omen denoting trust, faith and a happy outcome.

Anger: If the dreamer is himself the object of anger — he is much loved. If he himself is angry with a friend — that friend is especially true.

Arrow: If the dreamer is wounded — a confidence will be betrayed. If the dreamer is himself shooting arrows — he must beware of uttering lies and slander in the future.

Attic: This means a renewal of an old and trusted friendship. This also means you will move away from your present abode to a busy play where, if you are not married, you will meet your future partner.

Baby: For a woman — great joy and a true love coming. If a man dreams he is nursing a baby — a bitter disappointment in love awaits him.

Bachelor: To talk to a bachelor means there will be a wedding soon — but for a married man to dream he is again a bachelor is the warning of his future unfaithfulness.

Bagpipes: To hear them signifies the breaking of a true friendship or the loss of a dear friend.

Balcony: To watch others on a balcony denotes future success in love — to see the balcony give way or to be standing on it when it does, means a bitter quarrel with your lover.

Baldness: Someone close to you will suffer great loss or illness.

Ball: To be playing means exceptionally good news, but to watch others playing means the dreamer will be jealous of a friend.

Barefoot: To dream you are a beggar or are dressed in rags with bare feet, means that considerable sacrifices will be asked of you in marriage, but the result will be well worthwhile.

Bathing: If the water is clear, your love affair will end happily. If it is dirty or muddy, there will be unexpected troubles surrounding your love life.

Beans: To eat them brings sickness and misfortune. To see them grow — lovers' quarrels.

Beard: If a woman dreams she has grown a beard — she will soon be free of the attentions of an undesirable suitor.

Bed: To dream you are in bed means that you have a period of hectic activity ahead of you in which you will advance your interests satisfactorily. To dream you are in a strange bed, means that you will have to travel to attain your object or ambition, but there will be a period of strain before you can set off on your travels.

Bells: Tolling bells bring bad news of a friend or distant relation but a bell which is silent signifies a sudden quarrel between married people.

Bier: A contrary dream. A happy omen denoting a fortunate marriage in the family.

Birth: The end of one chapter or love affair, the start of another.

Blind Man: If you are leading the blind person your trust is being betrayed by one you love. If you yourself are blind — your choice of a future mate will be unfortunate.

Bread: To be eating bread signifies good health — but to be baking it denotes domestic troubles ending in quarrels.

Broom: To sweep with a broom denotes a great change in the life and occupation of the dreamer. To see a broom lying on the ground means the desertion of an old friend.

Bull: This is a warning that if you are too impetuous you will lose the person you have set your heart on.

Burial: This is a contrary dream, denoting good news which will affect your future coming from a relative.

Burns: If the dreamer is burnt, he will shortly receive a cash present; but if someone else is burnt, the dreamer will shortly meet a new and faithful friend.

Butterfly: You are warned that your lover is fickle.

Cage: If the dreamer is a woman and the cage is full of birds, she will soon be offered marriage, and if it is empty it denotes family opposition and an elopement or secret marriage in consequence. If the dreamer is a man, it foretells an early marriage.

Cards: If you are playing and know you will win, you will have a speedy marriage. If you lose, there will be danger ahead and if you are a spectator there will be an attempt to defraud you.

Cat: To dream of a cat either means deceit from a loved or a lucky meeting at night, depending on the sensation either of revulsion or affection you feel in your dream for the animal.

Chess: A bad dream for friendship — denoting the loss of friends and the gaining of new enemies.

Children: A happy dream. For a woman a good husband; for a man — domestic felicity.

Cinders: If the cinders glow, you will be loved by a warm generous person you have not met. If cold — your lover will not return your affection.

Clock: To see a clock means a cherished dream is coming nearer. To hear one strike means a proposal is imminent.

Clothes: If you are well-dressed, you will suffer the loss of money. If clothed in black — a great joy awaits you. If in white — much sorrow. However, if you see yourself in rags — your success is assured.

Cocks: If he crows, you have a false friend, plotting to do you harm. If he is silent, beware — for you have a rival in love who is more powerful than he seems.

Coffin: A contrary dream foretelling a recovery from illness and the disappearance of worries. If you dream you are lying in a coffin — either your sister or a very close friend will make an early marriage.

Cuckoo: If you hear but do not see the bird — someone will deliberately try to advise you wrongly. If you see the bird but it is silent — this denotes the arrival of a new love. But if it is singing, there will be quarrels and troubles with the old love before you meet the new.

Dancing: To dream you are dancing means you will receive an unexpected present from a stranger. To dance alone denotes a single life; and to watch others dancing denotes jealousy in love.

Deer: If the deer runs away, you will offend a loved one deeply. If the deer comes towards you, there will be a reconciliation with a former lover.

Dentist: To dream of having a tooth pulled means a money loss. To dream of having a tooth filled means someone will lend you money. But to dream of false teeth or a hollow tooth means a worrying situation will be brought into the open.

Digging: To dig for gold or treasure means lovers' quarrels, but to dig on a cultivated patch denotes your labours will bring you wealth.

Dining: For a spinster or bachelor this dream foretells an unhappy marital experience ending in separation or divorce. For a married person it denotes quarrels.

Dove: To see it fall means the death of a former love or relative, but to see it flying is a dream of positive happiness, peace and prosperity.

Drinking: To dream you are drunk denotes outstanding success. To dream of drinking alcohol denotes business losses, but the gain of a staunch ally. However, to dream you are drinking water means a bitter disappointment to your marital partner or lover.

Drowning: A fortunate dream if you yourself are drowning, meaning a service rendered to you which will bring you wealth. If you are watching others drown, this signifies misfortune through dalliance — but if you rescue them this means you will be lucky in love.

Drums: To hear drums means family quarrels — to see them silent means a reconciliation.

Eagle: Flying high means hopes come true — but if the bird is resting or comes to earth the lover will meet with a disillusionment.

Eating: Strife between friends and lovers.

Entertainment: Even when not allied to the former dream, this means broken contracts in love and commerce.

Exile: To be banished signifies discontent and the urge to travel. If friends are banished there will be domestic discord.

Eyes: Sore and infected eyes mean the illness of a lover or close friend. Blindness denotes the loss of these.

Fairy: Good news coming unexpectedly — but to the lover a most fortunate dream denoting a long and romantic association.

Farm: Great success encompassing much study. To the lover this foretells an early and happy marriage to a devoted partner.

Fingernails: To dream of having them cut, or of short nails, is a dream signifying dishonour, disgrace and estrangement from friends — but if your nails are unusually long this denotes success in business and love affairs.

Flowers: To dream of gathering flowers denotes a lovely surprise. Most flowers appertain to love. Withered flowers are contrary — meaning your troubles are not at an end. Red flowers are especially happy, denoting lasting friendships and happy marriages; white flowers usually presage unhappy love affairs and disappointments. However, for those who do not dream in colour, the following flowers have certain meanings:

Anemone:	You have a faithful lover.
Arum lily:	Unhappiness in marriage.
Bluebell:	Your marriage partner will be a scold.
Buttercup:	Your business affairs will prosper.
Carnation:	A passionate affair is imminent.
Clover:	Someone who has little money but a good heart will want to marry you.

Crocus:	A dark man will prove a deceiver.
Daffodil:	You have been unfair and unjust to a lover — seek a reconciliation.
Forget-me-nots:	Do not vacillate — but break off the harmful association at once.
Geranium:	You are worrying about a little quarrel that has been forgotten.
Honeysuckle:	Domestic quarrels.
Iris:	A letter will come to you with good news from your lover.
Marigold:	A failure in business through too much dalliance.
Peony:	Your modesty is excessive and will spoil your future prospects.
Poppy:	A message is coming which will cause great disappointment.
Primrose:	A new friendship will bring you contentment.
Rose:	Within a year a wedding — possibly your own.
Snowdrop:	It would be better if you confided your secret to someone you could trust.
Violet:	Your true love will be younger than you are.

Fortune Teller: To dream of a fortune teller, particularly of looking into a crystal, means there are hidden things or hidden enemies in your life which will be revealed to you in the nick of time.

Frog: A lucky dream for the lover — meaning a happy marriage.

Fruit: Most fruits symbolize abundance and prosperity — some have meanings appertaining to love.

Apricot:	Early marriage for the single — affectionate children for the married.
Cherry:	Denotes unhappy circumstances in romantic affairs.
Gooseberry	Be warned — you have a rival.
Grape:	Success in business — but jealousy for those in love.
Lemon:	Marital quarrels, separation and broken engagements.
Mulberry:	Through weakness and indecision you will lose a lover.

Orange:	A very unlucky dream denoting loss through a chance acquaintance and the loss of a lover through his or her infidelity.
Peach:	A lucky dream — love is reciprocated — good health and prosperity.
Pear:	A new romantic friendship.
Raspberry:	Consolation from an unexpected source after a great disappointment.
Strawberry:	You will visit new rural areas with a lover.

Funeral: A contrary dream denoting a marriage either of the dreamer or someone dear to them.

Garden: Marriage with a physically beautiful person.

Gloves: To lose them means business losses. To find a pair denotes a parting from a lover. If you wear them you will attend a wedding.

Grave: Another contrary dream meaning — lovers for the loveless; health and happiness where there has been sickness and poverty.

Guests: A crowd of unwanted guests means your luck will come unexpectedly. To dream of guests is a happy augury, and if you yourself are the guest then you will travel to far away places and your life will be changed from that time.

Gun: To fire a gun means a rival will triumph — but if someone else fires the gun, there will be a quarrel with an admirer.

Hammer: The sound of a hammer to a woman means she will marry a very busy man who will expect her to be a backstop in his business.

Heel: Denotes a minor lovers's quarrel.

Honey: A lucky dream meaning that the troubles of the past are now smoothing away and you can look forward to a long happy married life, and a good provider.

Horns: If you dream you have grown horns you will not marry for love.

Horse: To ride a horse means good friends in life and good money-making ability. To beat a horse denotes frustration of hopes and wishes. To see a number means independence and happiness and to fall off a horse depicts a hasty marriage. If you dream of white horses running, a wonderful lover awaits you. However, if you fall from the horse or cannot mount it, then your affair will be passionate but short lived.

Horseshoe: By contrary belief, this dream means gambling losses and unrequited love.

Hounds: If you are following them, it means you will reap success in love and marriage, but to be pursued by them means your marriage will be unhappy.

House: A new or strange dwelling means a contented spouse and domestic peace. To watch a house be demolished or fall signifies family discord and estrangements.

Husband: To dream of a husband when single means you will never marry. To dream of loving a friend's husband means that in reality that you are trying to hide the fact that you dislike him.

Hymn: If you are singing hymns your love will never be returned.

Ice: To those in love an ominous dream meaning the end of a relationship.

Ivory: Prosperity to the businessman and great future happiness to the lover.

Ivy: You will receive support and aid from a faithful friend.

Jealousy: To dream you are jealous means there will be cause later for you to be jealous — to dream someone else is jealous means you are truly loved.

Jewellery:　If the dreamer has passed through a great grief this is a happy dream meaning consolation from the love and devotion of another. For the lover this is not favourable — it means vanity will spoil many a romance.

Jigsaw:　To dream of playing with a jigsaw means you will overcome great restrictions which have been impeding your career or progress with a lover.

Key:　To dream of a single key denotes love and marriage — but to see a bunch means wealth but very little love. A discreditable dream warning that an alliance lightly entered into will bring discredit upon the dreamer.

Kissing:　To kiss someone against their will means your lover is true — but if you yourself resent being kissed you will live without love.

Knocking:　To dream you are knocking or hammering on a door for entrance means that you are committed to a hopeless cause and will only waste your life.

Lamp:　To dream of holding up a lighted lamp is a dream of comfort — where there has been sorrow and grief there will be joy. But to dream you are holding an unlighted lamp or candle means that you yourself are impeding your own progress by self pity and envy.

Love:　To the lonely and single — an affair of the heart, possibly marriage. But to the engaged and married this dream is unlucky, signifying quarrels. To see others in love means you will quarrel with or become indifferent to these people.

Magpie:　An omen of a hasty and unhappy union. To dream of two or more magpies is unlucky, for it means there will be a death around the house. One magpie means a sudden betrothal; two magpies for a woman mean a wealthy husband.

Marriage:　It is unlucky to dream of marriages or weddings; it signifies anxieties, burdens and tribulations.

Merry-Go-Round: Life will become easier and more organized in the future if you dream of riding on a merry-go-round. However, if you dream you are in a deserted fairground and the merry-go-round is empty but still revolving, then your troubles are mainly your own fault and unless you do some serious thinking your energies will be frittered uselessly away.

Moon: A new moon means unexpected happiness in love. A full moon means an approaching marriage.

Moths: To dream of moths is a warning that you are being led astray by happy-go-lucky company and both your reputation and your health will suffer.

Mouse: Busybodies will try to interfere with your romantic affairs.

Nest: An empty nest means distress, but eggs or fledgelings denote domestic happiness and a new abode.

Nose: To dream you have a large nose means future success in business and a happy marriage.

Nun: To those in trouble — consolation; to lovers — great happiness.

Nursery: Wealth and prosperity through honest labour. To the married — a direct prophecy meaning a birth; to those in love — an early engagement and wedding.

Nut: To dream you are eating nuts means you will bring your marriage partner to ruin through your own extravagance. But if you see them growing, your marriage partner will grow richer through the years.

Oar: To dream of only one oar or of losing an oar means the loss of a lover or good friend. To see a broken oar means a bitter quarrel.

Ocean
If the ocean is rough it denotes turbulence in the household. If it is smooth you will reconcile two lovers who have been parted, and if the moon is shining, you will find love yourself.

Organ: To dream you are yourself playing this instrument means advancement in career and a happy love affair.

Oyster: This predicts a luxurious and wealthy marriage.

Paper: When blank, there is a period of grief to be endured. Paper when it bears writing denotes great joy in connection with a love affair.

Path: A broad smooth path means extravagance, conceit and unhappy love affairs; a narrow, rough and crooked path denotes success in life and love.

Pawnbroker: To dream you are pawning something means that you are wasting your time with a person who is self obsessed and cannot return a genuine friendship or love.

Pigeon: When flying, good news can be expected from a long distance. When roosting, domestic harmony with a faithful partner.

Plough: To a man — prosperity through his own endeavours. To a woman — great domestic happiness.

Quail: An unlucky dream denoting many selfish love affairs causing great unhappiness.

Quarrelling: This is a contrary dream meaning reconciliation in love.

Quarry: A bad dream for those in love, signifying misunderstanding and estrangement.

Quicksands: A lucky dream predicting a wealthy marriage, if you yourself are sinking. If you see others sinking, it denotes opposition in business.

Race: To dream you are taking part in a race means you will shortly be faced with a serious temptation.

Rainbow: A bright rainbow foretells a brilliant marriage to someone who is famous and widely popular.

Raven: Many disappointments ahead — a serious loss of money and a rival in your affections. An unlucky dream denoting that you are surrounded by flatterers and deceit.

Reaping: Watching others reap means you will lose through extravagance. But if you yourself are reaping your career will prosper and marriage will eventuate within a year.

Ring: If a wife dreams she has broken a ring she will have a bitter quarrel with her husband.

Rival: To dream of a rival in love and business means you will succeed in all your aims.

River: Smooth flowing denotes love and happy quickmoving events. Turbulence means disturbances and misunderstanding. To dream you swim across a river or stream — your marriage partner will be fickle and nagging.

Rope: To dream you are bound by a rope means you will break a promise to a friend. To see others bound — you will be let down yourself.

Safe: An empty safe means an early marriage; a full safe, a late marriage. But if you dream you are breaking open a safe, you will not marry the person with whom you are now in love.

Scent: A bad omen of jealousy and lovers' quarrels, but promise of reconciliation.

Scissors: To a married person, a misunderstanding with the spouse.

But to the single, an approaching wedding.

Shark: A warning of a destructive person or force who will try to ruin your domestic peace.

Shaving: To dream someone is shaving you denotes an unfaithful lover.

Sheep: A flock feeding signifies a faithful lover — one single sheep, a disappointment in love.

Shield: To the young and single this promises the love and protection of someone famous and much honour and fame in their careers.

Shirt: To dream of a torn shirt means malicious lies have been circulated about you.

Sick: An omen of good fortune and love.

Silver: A dream which predicts the marriage of a relative or close friend.

Singing: Unlucky for the lover. Sudden disturbing news can be expected.

Snail: A dream both good and bad, denoting an upsetting conversation with a loved one, but also a letter bearing good news.

Snow: A dream, to an unmarried young girl, meaning she will shortly meet the man she will marry.

Sparrow: Great domestic felicity, if you dream you are feeding them. But if they fly away from you, an unpleasant surprise to do with domestic conditions awaits you.

Stars: A lucky dream if the stars are bright — great success in love and business. But if dim or fading the converse applies.

Stockings: Unlucky for men denoting ruin through extravagance. But for a woman it means conquests in love.

Swallows: One whom you have loved in the past will come back into your life again, and the outcome will be up to you as to whether he stays or flies away again.

Swan: If black — a handsome marriage partner. If white — a happy marriage and several children.

Teeth: To dream your teeth are being extracted, you will lose a friend. To dream they are blackened, broken or aching — a slight illness awaits you.

Thistle: A sign of disloyalty in a friend you trusted.

Tiger: A warning. Someone is coming into your life who will try to harm you.

Tower: To dream you are on top of a tower means a complete reversal in your financial affairs and a great romance.

Traveller: To be a traveller in a dream means that new horizons will open up for you soon. You have been in a rut. If you meet another traveller, then a person will come into your life who will be instrumental in freeing you from certain irksome conditions and showing you a new path.

Trees: Fruit trees mean great prosperity. Trees in bud mean a new love. Trees with luxuriant foliage mean a fruitful and happy marriage. Bare trees mean marital discord.

Trumpet: To see a trumpet but not hear it means a great disappointment. But to hear it means your lover or friend is insincere in his affections.

Turtle: Great mutual happiness and love.

Uniform: A journey full of adventure will occur and will have a special romantic interest.

Valley: To dream you are looking down a valley means you will have cause to regret past actions. To walk or stand in a valley means a new dwelling and a meeting with an old friend.

Veil: To a woman, if she is veiled and the veil is torn, this means a secret will be revealed — but if others are wearing veils there will be many misunderstandings between lovers and friends.

Vinegar: The dreamer is warned his jealous nature will cause trouble.

Violin: A dream, for lovers, meaning an early marriage and prosperity.

Wasp: To dream you are stung by a wasp means enemies will try to injure you.

Water: To drink clear refreshing water — an early marriage. To drink bad tasting water — misfortune.

Weapons: Beware of false friends who are betraying you.

Weeping: A contrary dream denoting joy and laughter.

Wheat: To the lover — the person of his or her choice.

Widow: If a spinster dreams she is a widow, she will soon marry. If a wife dreams she is bereaved — her husband will live long and prosper.

Wife: If a spinster dreams of being a wife she will never marry. Should a husband dream of his wife — she is faithful and devoted.

Wig: To dream that you are wearing a wig means that you will meet someone who does not wear his heart on his sleeve, but will be genuine. To dream of your lover wearing a wig means that he is desirous of making a change in his career, but lacks the confidence to make the break, or fears your disapproval.

Window: To dream of watching from a window means a reconciliation. To see someone watching you through a window denotes slander directed towards you.

Wings: To dream you have grown wings, you can expect melancholy news concerning a lover.

Witch: A lucky dream bringing solutions to problems and a discovery.

Wolf: You have a treacherous friend ready to discredit you.

Women: If a woman dreams of seeing other women, she will have many new clothes. If a man dreams of seeing women he will be surrounded by lies, by betrayal, and can expect a love affair or marriage to finish badly.

Wounds: A favourable dream to young lovers promising success.

Wreath: For the older person this dream means longstanding problems will be solved. For the younger, it means happy love affairs.

Writing: To watch another write a letter means a violent quarrel. To write a letter yourself means you will receive one from a dear friend.

Yoke: A sign of approaching nuptials; yours, if single — a dear friend's, if you are married.

Signs of the Zodiac: The dreamer will travel a great deal and will eventually marry and settle in a foreign country.

CHAPTER 10

Love in a Teacup

One of the simplest ways of foretelling the future is by reading tea leaves. It does not need any special skill or psychic knowledge, just an open mind, imagination and the ability to interpret the facts.

There is an elaborate ritual connected with tea leaf reading which in my opinion was devised to impress the sitter with the solemnity and significance of the ceremony. It is not at all necessary to turn the cup three times around and then upend it.

You will need a wide mouthed cup, white on the inside, and a good brand of tea that does not deteriorate into dust. China tea is traditionally the best to use for this purpose.

All you will need to remember is that the handle of the cup is known as the 'house' or dwelling of the person wanting the cup read, or the sitter or enquirer as he or she is known. Events happening near this 'house' are coming into the home or affecting the people therein. Things which are seen further away, either in the middle or at the bottom can either minimize a benefit or an unfortunate omen or mean a distance in time. All symbols must be taken together: it is seldom a single symbol is read alone, so that the presence of hearts, crosses, money dots, roadway dots or other attendant symbols contribute to the final interpretation. Large dark clumps of tea leaves are never good omens, but there could be mitigating factors present in the other tea leaf pictures. You will definitely see pictures if you concentrate, and in time you can learn to interpret them accurately, always realizing that the little extra sense we all possess is lying dormant waiting for you to bring it out and polish it up.

I have selected the signs pertaining to the affairs of the heart, but don't forget that the position of this sign, near the handle of 'house' or at the bottom of the cup has a great bearing upon its significance and strength.

Let's look at the placing of the signs more carefully. Should the sign be near the handle or 'house' it is often sudden and sometimes unfortunate; should it be at the bottom of the cup, then it will take longer to come to pass. Should the heart or symbol be ringed around with small dots, then the way will be stormy and many troubles will beset the course of this romance. If a heart or ring is near a cross or the head of a dog or horse then there will be the death of a beloved friend, and should a heart or any symbol meaning romance be placed at the end of a straight succession of small dots, the symbol for a roadway, then romance will be found at the end of a long journey. If a dollar or pound sign is seen money will be present. Should a ship appear near the symbol of romance, this could mean that either the object of the romance will be connected with the sea, or the person concerned will meet his or her fate on a ship, and as a ship is a good omen this romance will be lucky. These signs must be read in accord with all the other signs in the teacup, and interpreted by the reader in the light of his knowledge of traditional meanings.

Firstly we will start with symbols of good omen. If these are present, success will be assured in both romantic *and* commercial affairs.

Signs of Good Omen

Acorn; anchor; angel; basket of flowers; bee; boot; bouquet; bridge; bull; circle; clover; corn; cornucopia; cow; daffodil; dog; dove; duck; eagle; elephant; fish; garland of flowers; horseshoe; horse; oak; palm; rose; ship; swan; talisman.

We will have to include symbols of bad omen as these could be found near a symbol of romance and would act as a warning.

Symbols of Bad Omen

Arc; bat; clouds; coffin; dagger; drum; flag (black); gun; hour glass; monkey; mouse; owl; rat; raven; scythe; skeleton; skull; snake; spear; square; sword; wreck.

There is more than one meaning for some symbols, depending upon where they are placed. For instance, a gun, although deemed unfortunate in some circumstances, can also mean sudden news. Bells and flying birds can also mean news, although they also can stand for other events.

Because they are necessary to determine whether the romance will be happy and fulfilled, or dangerous and destructive for the enquirer, it is necessary first to give the meanings of the Good and Evil Omens, then to deal with the many symbols appertaining to love, courtship and domestic felicity.

Symbols of Good Omen and Their Meaning

Acorn: Good fortune in money matters at the top, health and happiness in the middle of the cup, and at the bottom continued improvement in health and happiness.

Anchor: If found at the top, constancy in love and success in commercial enterprise; if found in the middle, particularly if surrounded by small dots in orderly lines, a voyage which will bring prosperity; and at the bottom, a voyage linked with love. However, if seen with clouds or encircled by short lines this symbol and all others must be read in reverse.

Angel: Fortunate indeed for the lover, this emblem means news from a loved one which could change your life.

Basket of Flowers: If there is a ring or bell near this symbol it denotes new happiness, new engagements; if no ring is present, then a pleasurable meeting could later lead to marriage; it will be in your hands.

Bee: A symbol in the cup of industry and prudence, and to the lover good news which will bring the end of any serious financial worry.

Boot: A lucky symbol, if well defined, bringing protection both spiritual and material. However, if the boot is ragged, then disgrace will follow. If at the top, the boot suggests a wandering nature; if in the middle there will be hidden danger, particularly if the boot is ill formed; and if at the bottom, particularly if a ring or heart is seen close by, there will be a wedding.

Bouquet: This sign is one of the luckiest, as it completely nullifies any unfortunate signs found in the cup and signifies success, staunch friends and wealth. To the lover it means a happy marriage.

Bridge: This symbol is lucky, meaning that shortly there will arise for you the opportunity of a lifetime which should be grasped immediately for it will lead to great happiness. When surrounded by dashes, it means you will escape great danger.

Bull: A good sign meaning prosperity and health and the trampling of all opposition underfoot.

Circle: A reassuring sign that denotes all projects will be completed favourably; but if a line is drawn through the middle, parting and separation are predicted.

Clover: A shamrock or clover is an emblem of good fortune. It immediately nullifies all other signs of evil omen in the cup. Depending upon its position in the cup, the good fortune will be either slow in coming or immediate.

Corn: This is the symbol of prosperity, and when seen near the handle or 'house' it means there will be a very special festive gathering.

Cornucopia: Peace, prosperity and plenty will attend if you have this symbol in your cup.

Cow: Another symbol of prosperity and increase in possessions. If the head of the cow is turned away from the 'house' or handle of the cup, your wealth will come from overseas. To the farmer a particularly favourable sign.

Daffodil: Like all flowers, the daffodil means happiness and pleasant things in a cup. This flower means success as well and pleasure, but if found at the bottom of the cup, it is a warning not to fritter too much of your wealth or talents in the search for pleasure.

Dog: The symbol of faithful friendship and help from friends. Your friends will prove true in adversity and you will receive much help and advice from them. If found at the bottom of the cup a friend will need help, and if seen begging you will receive an urgent request for help.

Dot: Strengthens attendant symbols. A number of small dots represents money.

Dove: This is the universal symbol of domestic peace and happiness. A favourable sign appertaining to the purchase or possession of a new home and a new way of life.

Duck: This symbol, though particularly fortunate to the farmer, means an increase in material prosperity due to exchange or barter.

Eagle: Although this is a fortunate symbol, it is a lonely and powerful one meaning that you will rise to great heights, have the envy of lesser men, and know few true friends. There is a warning that conceit could be your downfall.

Elephant: This is a good luck emblem, but it also means attainment over a period of time, by slow and sure methods. It gives wisdom and physical and moral strength to the enquirer. If however it is seen in outline only, then there will be a warning that you are paying too much attention to worldly matters to the detriment of your spiritual welfare.

Fish: One of the very luckiest you may observe in a cup, this symbol nullifies every evil condition and gives success, peace and plenty. If surrounded by small dots, then the luck will be financial.

Flowers: One flower means a kind thought or action done for you. A bouquet of small flowers means gracious praise from a sincere person.

Garland: This symbol means high honours and success, in both work and friendship.

Horse: If galloping, then news from a beloved friend. The head of a horse denotes a lover and if it is well defined so are his affections; if broken or shadowy, his heart is not true. A rider on a horse denotes wonderful news from abroad, and a horse standing means that your work will be for the betterment of the community, and that you are endowed with sagacity, wisdom and faithfulness in your career.

Horseshoe: A good luck surprise in store for you. If dots are near it, then money is involved, and when found near the 'house' then love and courtship are involved.

Oak: Great strength of character is yours if an oak tree or leaf is seen in your cup, and many will be the burdens brought to you by others in your long and prosperous life.

Palm: You will be crowned with honour and respect.

Rose: A lucky sign and emblem of true friendship, happiness and success. To the artist, it promises high honour; to the lover it speaks of a long happy wedded life, and to all it denotes that the time has now come to embark on long cherished new projects. However, if withered, it means the decline of love.

Ship: A very lucky symbol, a steam ship or sailing barque, if clearly defined. However, if the ship is badly formed or the sails are tattered then there will be a reversal of fortune. Prosperity, health and assured wealth are on their way to you if the ship is pointing to the 'house' and possibly visitors or news from overseas, but if it points away from the handle then a journey will occur. Two ships mean increase in trade or business.

Swan: A smooth graceful progress with no storms to mar the way to your happiness is foretold by this symbol. A quiet way of life is indicated; and if a heart or ring is nearby a faithful steady lover and a happy calm marriage is indicated.

Talisman: Any good luck sign, such as a swastika, seal of Solomon or anchor means that you are protected by occult influences at this period in your life.

Symbols of Bad Omen
Keep in mind that these can be mitigated by other more fortunate symbols, and most of these serve as a warning to the enquirer, so that unfortunate events can either be changed by direct action or their impact lessened by preparedness.

Arc: This is a symbol of unforeseen happenings, broken careers, unfinished projects, usually through no fault of the enquirer.

Bat: This is a warning that you have to beware of secret enemies who will work in the dark so that your efforts will be fruitless, unless you learn to be more circumspect in your choice of friends and examine each one closely for signs of envy and malice.

Clouds: Troubles of a minor nature are represented by clouds. If dots are seen nearby then the trouble will be financial. If the clouds are seen at the bottom of the cup they you will receive news of a severe illness. If the entire cup looks cloudy and confused, then your mind is so unsettled that it is wiser to postpone the reading until you are feeling more positive and settled.

Coffin: This sign is not a sign of death but of illness brought on by neglect. It is a warning to safeguard your health. When surrounded by small dots it means a failure in business.

Cross: This is the symbol of suffering. Two crosses, a severe illness or affliction. You will have to overcome great trials and troubles and self sacrifice will be your portion, but eventually if you have purity of heart and great determination you will win through.

Dagger: Secret blows from enemies who are envious and treacherous and who will try to damage your reputation or your business. A warning to examine your friends' motives very carefully.

Drum: The symbol of scandal and a public attack on your integrity, this symbol if near the 'house' means domestic discord through lying tongues. If more than one drum is seen then there will be riots.

Flag: Wounds in war are foretold. If the flag is black, then you will hear of the death of a soldier.

Gun: An attack from a long distance. If it is at the bottom of the cup, the attack will come in the form of slanderous gossip, while if it is near the 'house' it will affect your domestic circle. If a heart is seen near it then there will be damage to your affections. It can also mean sudden news, not necessarily unpleasant, depending upon which other symbols are seen near it.

Hour Glass: If seen near the handle, this tells of some domestic tragedy due to lack of foresight; if at the bottom of the cup, then danger will arise through neglected behaviour. It is a warning also that time is on the wing, and that procrastination is present. You should see that each task is finished before commencing another and be careful not to diffuse your energies too much.

Monkey: There will be people who flatter or imitate you, but they will be insincere and cause much mischief, so beware of them.

Mouse: This is the symbol of poverty through neglect of opportunities and timidity. If seen near the 'house' then there will be a theft. It is a warning to 'get up and go', and seek your avenues of employment and opportunity.

Owl: A warning that unless all precautions are taken there will be a failure of health and business. If seen near the top of the cup near the handle, misery and sorrow through the unfaithful conduct of a loved one or lover.

Rat: This is the symbol of treachery and malice. You will suffer a loss through trusting unwisely. It would be better if you did not underestimate your enemies, and on no account turn your back upon them, for they will be very vindictive.

Raven: This is a mischievous symbol, not a very harmful one. If a raven or crow or rook if seen in the cup, it means that you lack a settled aim in life and that you also tend to profit at others' expense. You must learn to rely on your own talents and to cultivate stability of habits. If seen near the handle or 'house', then there will be unpleasant gossip and if found at the bottom of the cup, then a suit for slander is imminent.

Scorpion: This is the symbol of vindictive enemies and denotes that your advance must be slow and cautious.

Scythe: This unfortunate symbol denotes the cutting off or trampling underfoot of cherished plans, the sudden ending of a business concern, or the failure of health. Near the 'house', it denotes the illness or sudden trouble of a relative while at the bottom, it means a severe illness arising from an accident.

Skull: Avoid unnecessary risks, for danger lies in your path. Take better care of yourself.

Snake: The symbol of enmity and plotting: be warned, for one of your enemies is getting ready to strike. If found near the 'house', one of your domestic circle is a snake in the grass in whom your trust is misplaced.

Spear: A sudden assault of an enemy. You are very sensitive to others and must strengthen yourself, for there will be harsh words said soon which will upset you.

Square: This symbol indicates either physical or mental restriction and if surrounded by small dots, a financial restriction of great magnitude. It can also mean imprisonment or the forced cessation of activities through illness. Also, you must guard your tongue, or you will trap yourself through slander of others with serious consequences.

Sword: Be on your guard, for this symbol means the sudden onslaught of an enemy. A broken sword means a victory for your opponents.

Wreck: Disaster threatens your affairs. If surrounded by small dots, then there will be financial crash; if a heart or ring is seen near it, then the dissolution of a marriage, particularly if it is found near the handle.

Now we come to the general symbols of love, courtship, marriage and family life. Once again the position in the cup must be taken into account as well as the presence of good or bad omens, and whether the symbols are clearly drawn, solid or outlined. Rest assured that if you see one or more of those symbols in the tea cup then the enquirer will meet romance in his or her life in the very near future, be it for good or ill, as only the cup can show.

The Lovers' Symbols

Ace of hearts: There will be an important decision made in the near future in regard to your homelife, affecting you and someone you love.

Anchor: At the top of the cup, constancy and success in love and success in commercial enterprise; if found in the middle, particularly if surrounded by small dots in orderly lines, a voyage which will bring prosperity; and at the bottom a voyage linked with love. However, if seen with clouds or encircled by short lines this symbol and all others must be read in reverse.

Angel: Good news for the lover from the object of his or her affections. Fortunate indeed for the lover, this emblem means news from a loved one which could change your life.

Apple: All fruit is lucky. Your lover will be a person desiring knowledge. That knowledge will bring great honour and gain.

Arrow: When seen bisecting a heart or near a heart, the enquirer will make a sudden complete romantic attachment.

Badger: If the enquirer is an unmarried man, this symbol denotes a long bachelorhood, possibly lifelong.

Ball: To a lover this symbol means he or she must try to stop taking the line of least resistance.

Bed: The symbol of the state of mind of the enquirer, always vital to the lover. If the bed is tidily made then ease and happiness through an ordered mind will result; if the bed is untidy, then a disordered mind and life is foretold.

Bells: Only if two bells are seen together does this mean a wedding which will bring happiness and wealth. One bell means news. If near a cross — bereavement.

Birds: Birds flying near a heart denote good news from a lover. Love birds on a bough denote peace in love and love birds fighting means lovers' quarrels that are not lasting.

Bond: If a connecting link can be seen between two like symbols, then two people will be drawn into a strong and permanent union, which can be either love, friendship or business.

Boot: If this symbol is attended by a heart, then a wedding is imminent.

Bouquet: Nullifying any trouble which may occur, this symbol denotes a happy and prosperous marriage.

Bow (Ribbon) or Lovers' Knot: If this is seen, it denotes a new love interest, and when with a heart, it will end in marriage.

Bracelet: This is another symbol of union, meaning either business or romance, but there is a warning of servitude if the band is wide.

Butterfly: The symbol of the flirt and gadabout, it carries a warning not to fritter energies or money needlessly, but also is a symbol of much pleasurable social activity.

Cage: If the enquirer is a female and there is a ring within the cage and the cage is near the 'house' then there will be a wedding. If surrounded by dots, a wealthy marriage. If down at the bottom of the cup, a loveless marriage.

Cat: Seen near the handle or 'house', this symbol is of domestic peace.

Chain: If unbroken it denotes an early marriage. If broken then there will be either a business contract or an engagement or marriage broken in the near future.

Cradle: Near the handle, the birth of a baby; in the middle, new beginnings; at the bottom surrounded by clouds, the illness of a baby.

Dove: Favourable conditions pertaining to heart and home.

Face: If pleasant in profile, this is a good omen, meaning happiness through a new friend. If ugly or menacing, the opposite conditions prevail. If two faces are seen, there will be a new advantageous friendship.
Fan: The symbol of dissimulation and flirtation. If the fan is open the lover can expect deception on a grand scale from his beloved; if the fan is shut, there will be temporary deceit or falseness.
Feather: A warning sign to the lover that he is burning the candle at both ends and neglecting his work for his amours.
Fern: Inconstancy and wavering affection is denoted by this symbol. Restlessness and the wanderlust will bring trouble to the lover.
Fox: A warning to the enquirer that one of his friends is playing him false and could be a rival in the affairs of the heart.
Frog: A warning to a lover not to be too puffed up with conceit or he will lose his love.

Glove: A challenge will be thrown down to the lover and he will have to fight for his happiness.
Gun: If a heart is seen near this symbol then there will be news of a lover; if at the bottom of the cup, there will be damage to the affections.

Harp: Harmony is domestic affairs, success in social ventures and new friendships.
Hat: If a heart or ring is observed near this sign then a happy marriage will result.
Heart: The symbol of sincere affection. If seen at the end of a succession of small dots, you will meet love at the end of a journey. If two together, or there is a ring attendant, then there will be a wedding. If fruit can be seen near the heart, then there will be much lighthearted enjoyment. If near an initial, a new lover. If love birds, bells or lovers' knots are seen, a sure and happy wedding.
Heel: To the single person this is a clear statement that marriage would be the answer to his or her problems and that it will eventuate.
Horse: The head of a horse denotes the lover. If the head is well defined the lover is constant.

Horseshoe: If seen near the 'house' this is a lucky emblem to do with all matters of the heart.

House: To the lover this symbol means the realization of all his hopes and wishes.

Idol: A warning that your trust will soon be betrayed for you are mistaken in the character of the one you love.

Ivy: The symbol of faithfulness, and when seen near the 'house' means a devoted lover.

Kangaroo: Family affection and love are symbolized by this sign.

Key: If found near the 'house' it means domestic happiness and a new dwelling, but if two are seen then there is the danger of robbery.

Knife: If seen near the handle or 'house' this means a separation or divorce.

Lamb: A new young energetic lover will be yours in the spring.

Leaves: A happy second marriage.

Letter: News is coming to you from a lover, particularly if there is a heart placed close by. Sometimes there will also be an initial.

Lily: If this flower is seen near the handle or 'house', then there will be a virtuous marriage partner.

Mermaid: To the lover this symbol spells danger. There will be overwhelming attraction or temptation which could only lead to his or her destruction.

Moon: If a full moon is shown, then there will be a new love affair. If it is clearly defined then it will be very happy, and if dots surround it it may well be a marriage of convenience or a money match.

Mouse: Someone who loves you is waiting for you. Show more courage in your pursuit.

Mushroom: Symbolizing growth and expansion, there is a caution not to be too precipitate in your affairs, although the presence of a heart denotes a new love about to enter your life.

Nail: If seen near the 'house, a great injustice or hurt will be directed against one you love.

Necklace: If complete, this means the receipt of an honour, but if broken, there will be a loss in matters of the heart.

Nun: A sign of secrecy and deception on the part of a lover whom you have trusted in the past.

Owl: If near the 'house' and at the top of the cup then there will be great misery through the unfaithful conduct of a loved one.

Pansy: You are always in your friend's thoughts.

Peacock: A heart near this sign denotes a rich lover, and a ring means a wealthy and happy marriage. If seen near the 'house', then the home will be beautiful and luxurious.

Piano: A symbol of peace and harmony like the harp, this denotes that you will rule over a happy and peaceful house and help develop the talents of your offspring.

Pistol: A sudden decision through a threat. Beware of coercion to make you do something you know is morally wrong.

Priest: When seen near the 'house', this symbol can mean a marriage if a heart or ring are present, or a death if other signs are there.

Razor: If seen near a heart, this denotes a lovers' quarrel and even a separation.

Reins: This is a warning that you have reached the crossroads and must seek guidance, for events ahead of you will be of great import in your future life. You must learn not to let your heart rule your head.

Ring: The symbol of lasting friendship, it speaks of completion, eternity and earthly love.

Rose: The fulfilment of all the lover's hopes and wishes is assured by this emblem unless it is withered, for then so will be his hopes.

Sabot: The wooden shoe serves as a warning to lovers to broaden their outlook and be more forgiving or else they will lose their sweetheart.

Saw: Outside influences will try to destroy your domestic peace and harmony unless you are careful, particularly with new acquaintances.

Scales: Symbolizing justice, they denote that your actions are being weighed up, and you will be justly dealt with according to your deserts.

Scimitar: Your passions will get the better of you to your detriment unless you practise self control.

Scissors: Unhappiness and disputes through 'nagging and bickering'. If seen near the 'house' there will be domestic quarrels, and if near a heart then lovers will be separated by harsh words.

See-Saw: The course of your love affair will have many ups and downs before reaching its conclusion. Do not become disheartened.

Spider: Near the handle, perseverance in love; if in the middle or at the bottom, in-laws and enemies will try to make trouble for you.

Spoon: A spoon denotes a christening and two spoons mean a flirtation.

Stars: When seen as a group of small stars near the 'house', you can expect to have happy, talented and contented children.

Swan: If near a heart, a faithful lover, and if with a ring, a happy marriage.

Table: Denotes family celebration if under the handle.

Toad: If seen near the handle, this presages domestic trouble through deceit or flattery.

Turtle: The end of strife and quarrels in a love affair and the beginning of peace and harmony.

Vase: If near the handle, a productive union; if in the middle of the cup, it will take time and care to achieve; if found at the bottom or with clouds, attainment only after sacrifice.

Violet: If near a heart, then a modest, unassuming but true lover awaits you.

Volcano: A warning to be discreet and to keep a check on your passions, for lack of self control will surely bring trouble in its wake.

Weather Vane: If near a heart then a fickle lover is indicated as this is the symbol of inconstancy.

Wolf: A rival is intriguing against you. Take care.

Worm: Secret enemies try to undermine you with your loved one. Seek the truth boldly and confront them.

Wreck: If near the 'house' this signifies separation from the loved one.

Yoke: This symbol of slavery is a warning that you are losing your own personality and interests through the domination of another.

CHAPTER 11

Flower Language for Lovers

Long ago in the Orient and in Arabia flowers were used by lovers to convey poetical thoughts and romantic messages. This spread to medieval France and England. In time, each blossom came to have an ascribed meaning, and whole love-letters were contained in one small posy. In Victorian England, some ingenious lover, perhaps an even more enterprising florist, invented a floral clock so that lovers could plot secret messages giving both the time and place of meeting. From the more general flowery phrase there developed a specific, very much to the point, method of communication, known as Florigraphy, or, the language of flowers.

The Floral Clock

Glossary of Terms that Govern Clandestine
Lovers' Meetings

Meet me	= Ivy
Tonight	= White Campion
Today	= Pimpernel
Tomorrow	= Buttercup
Morning	= Bell Flowers
I Will Meet You	= Ivy and White Clover
I Cannot Meet You	= Ivy and Lavender
Make Another Appointment	= Ivy and Red Clover
Meet Me Tonight at Seven	= Ivy, White Campion and Sweet William

The Floral Clock

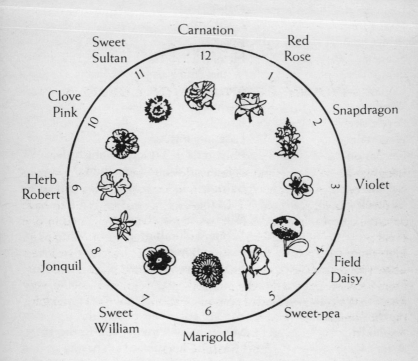

Hours of the Floral Clock

1 o'clock	Red Rose	7 o'clock	Sweet William
2 o'clock	Snapdragon	8 o'clock	Jonquil
3 o'clock	Violet	9 o'clock	Herb Robert
4 o'clock	Field Daisy	10 o'clock	Clove Pink
5 o'clock	Sweet-pea	11 o'clock	Sweet Sultan
6 o'clock	Marigold	12 o'clock	Carnation

General Terms to do With Clandestine Meetings.

Proximity	Petunia
Courage	Oak Leaves
Indecision	Golden Rod
Protection	Fever Few
Scandal	Hemlock
Temporization	White Poppy
Uselessness	Meadow-sweet
Warning	Fuchsia or Oleander
Animosity	Basil
Uncertainty	Love-in-a-mist
Deception	Phlyorcus or Deadly Nightshade
Impatience	Balsam or White Geranium
Rashness	Bulrush
Obstacles	Blackthorn
Truce	White Chrysanthemum
Folly	White Columbine
Denial	Passion-flower
Duplicity	Scarlet Geranium

Floral Vocabulary

Apple blossom	You are good and beautiful.
Asphodel	My regret will follow you to the grave.
Aster	I was too impetuous, I am having second thoughts.
Azalea	Please be more moderate in action.
Bachelor's button	I shall remain unwed.
Balm	It was only said in fun.
Balsam	Hurry, I can hardly wait to see you.
Bay-leaf	I shall never change.
Begonia	We are being watched;
Berry-flower	Meet me tomorrow morning.
Bitter-sweet	My words are sincere.
Black-thorn	There are many difficulties before us.
Bluebell	I am faithful.
Bracken	You enchant me.

Bramble	Forgive me for my hasty words.
Broom	I am always yours.
Bulrush	Please be more discreet.
Buttercup	How radiantly fresh you are.
Calceolaria	Please let me assist you financially.
Camellia	Your beauty is radiant.
Camomile	Hope on, you have shown great courage, despite many setbacks.
Campion (red)	I should like to meet you.
Campion (white)	Meet me in the evening.
Candy-tuft	My heart is untouched by you.
Canterbury bell (blue)	Do not listen to lies, I am yours.
Canterbury bell (white)	I received your gift and will treasure it dearly.
Carnation (pink)	Thank you for the charming token.
Carnation (red)	I must see you soon.
Carnation (white)	The love I offer is pure.
Cherry-blossom	To the ripening of our friendship.
Chrysanthemum (bronze)	I will be your friend but cannot love you.
Chrysanthemum (red)	I love you.
Chrysanthemum (white)	I believe in you.
Chrysanthemum (yellow)	My love is already given.
Cineraria	You are delightful company.
Cinquefoil	Please look on me as your family.
Clarkia	Your company and conversation are stimulating.
Clematis	Your have a brilliant intellect.
Clover (pink)	Do not flirt with me.
Clover (red)	Please remember me and be faithful while I am gone.
Clover (white)	I will be true.
Cocks-combs	Your efforts are wasted, I do not like you.
Columbine (purple)	Please forgive my folly, I shall never give you up.
Columbine (white)	You are being stupid, your attentions are unwelcome.

Coriander	Do not judge by first appearance.
Cornflower	My heart is not a fortress to be brutally stormed.
Cowslip	You are the breath of spring.
Crocus	My heart beats with yours.
Currant, Flowering	You are presumptuous, we have nothing in common.
Cyclamen	I am indifferent to you, and unmoved by your protestations.
Daffodil	I do not return your feelings.
Dahlia (red)	You have mistaken my feelings.
Dahlia (white)	Do not approach me again.
Dahlia (yellow)	Your attention are distasteful to me.
Daisy (common)	Let me wait a few days before giving an answer.
Daisy (Michaelmas)	I can never love you, please cease writing to me.
Daisy (moon)	Our ages are incompatible, you must look for one nearer to your own age.
Daisy (ox-eye)	I could learn to love you.
Dandelion	Your whole attitude is ridiculous.
Deadly Nightshade	You are false and are deceiving me.
Dog-rose	You are very beautiful.
Dog-violet	You are my first love.
Evening Primrose	Humbly I love you.
Everlasting Flower	I will go away as you wish but you will never be forgotten.
Fern-Maiden-hair	I am pure and heart whole, and you have a chance to win me.
Forget-me-not	Think of me while I am away from you.
Foxglove	You do not know the meaning of love.
Frankincense	My incense is that of a faithful heart.
Fuchsia	Beware — I carry a warning, your lover is deceiving you.

Gardenia	You are pure like this blossom.
Geranium (pink)	Please explain your actions.
Geranium (red)	I do not trust you.
Geranium (white)	I have come to no decision.
Gladiola	Your words hurt me very much.
Golden Rod	I have not made up my mind yet.
Guinea Flower	You are dear to my heart.
Hare-bell	I am resigned. I shall go away if that is what you want, but I still hold out hope.
Heliotrope	I adore you, you centre my universe.
Hollyhock	I could achieve great things with you at my side.
Honesty	I have been completely frank with you.
Hyacinth (blue)	I devote my life to your service.
Hyacinth (white)	I admire you.
Hydrangea	You are dreadfully fickle.
Iris (purple)	You have set fire to my heart.
Ivy	I want to be a bondsman to you.
Jasmine	How elegant your mind is.
Jonquil	Please answer my petition, may I hope for your love.
King-Cup	I wish I were better endowed with the world's riches.
Laburnum	Why have you neglected me?
Larkspur	You have been trifling with my affections. I demand an answer.
Lavender	Loving is not liking. I like you — that is all, I am sorry.
Lilac (purple)	You are my first love.
Lilac (white)	A tribute to your spiritual beauty and innocence.
Lily (Tiger)	I am passionately in love.

Lily (white)	You are so pure and unsullied. I kiss the hem of your gown.
Lily-of-the-valley	Do not speak of love, you confuse me: let us rather speak of friendship.
Lobelia (blue)	I don't love you, nor even like you.
London pride	I am sorry to have caused you pain. I was only flirting.
Love-in-a-mist	I cannot understand your message, please explain.
Lupin	You are over-bold. Go softly and you might have success.
Magnolia	Take good heart, things will be better in the future.
Marigold (African)	You are not refined but uncouth and insensitive.
Marigold (French)	Your unreasonable jealousy will spoil things between us.
Marjoram	You are frightening me.
Mignonette	You are worthy but dull.
Mimosa	I am sensitive and you are too brusque.
Mint	Better if you find a mate nearer to your age.
Mistletoe	I send you a thousand kisses and blessings.
Mock-orange	The wedding will be cancelled.
Musk	You are spoiling your natural charms by over-adornment.
Myrtle	Be my love.
Narcissus	I couldn't compete with you, you love yourself too much.
Nasturtium	I look for a natural beauty.
Oak-leaves	Love will find a way out of all difficulties.
Oleander	One of your false friends has betrayed our secret.

Orchid	I would love to give you all the luxuries you have never known.
Pansy (purple)	Our memories sustain me.
Pansy (white)	You are always on my mind.
Pansy (yellow)	I think of you always though we are absent one from the other.
Passionflower	I must renounce you for the sake of others.
Peach-blossom	Please let's not talk of love, and I shall be your friend.
Pelargonium	I am your slave, hear me. Please forgive me for my insensitivity.
Periwinkle	Until I saw you I knew not what love was.
Petunia	I like to be close to you always.
Phlox (pink)	We will be good friends.
Phlox (white)	I would like to know more about you.
Pimpernel	Please find a time and fix a place for our first meeting.
Pink-clove	How lovely you are.
Poppy (red)	Sudden tactics will get you nowhere, time and patience will win all.
Poppy (white)	I have not yet made up my mind.
Primrose	I could learn to love you.
Rocket	You have a rival for my affections.
Rose (Christmas)	I am in suspense and cannot bear it.
Rose (moss)	I love you from afar.
Rose (red)	I love you.
Rose (white)	I love you not.
Rose (yellow)	I love another.
Rosemary	Never will I forget you.
Saffron-flower	You abuse my regard for you.
Salvia (red)	Passion is often short-lived.
Saxifrage	Even a smile from you would reward me.
Shamrock	Where you are there shall be joy and laughter.

Snapdragon	You mean nothing to me.
Snowdrop	Once again I am bidding for your love.
Solomon's seal	I neither have riches nor am I handsome, but I dare to love you.
Sunflower	You cannot turn my head with ostentation.
Sweet-pea	You have left me sweet memories.
Sweet-Sultan	This is to wish you happiness.
Sweet-William	I was only teasing you.
Tansy	I am not interested.
Trumpet-flower	You are like a flame of fire.
Tuberose	I have seen a beautiful girl who has singed my wings.
Tulip	I declare my passion.
Tulip-tree	With your love I could achieve wealth and fame.
Verbena	You have bewitched me.
Veronica	You are my true love, till death do us part.
Violet	Sweet, shy and untouched you are.
Wallflower	I am constant to you always.
Wormwood	Partings are such sweet sorrows.

CHAPTER 12

Old Spells and Incantations

Here are some ancient spells for those anxious to meet their fate. These have come down to use through the centuries from legions of lovers and love-lorn maidens. A not inconsiderable part of their charm is the knowledge that human nature has always suffered and sought for love since the world began. While they are all fun to try, who knows . . . white magic may work for you . . . if you really believe.

To Find Out Whom You will Marry

The Pea-Pod Method
The pea-pod must have nine peas in it; you suspend it over a door by a white thread. If the next person who enters the door is not a member of the family, and is unmarried, then your wedding will take place in twelve months.

The Red Rose
Pluck a red rose during the month of June in England or in the U.S.A., (in December in Australia and Africa), before 7 a.m. and place it in an envelope. Seal the envelope with wax, with your ring finger, the third finger of the left hand. Now place it under your pillow and carefully note your dreams on the following night. If you do not dream, it can remain for seven nights. If your dreams are of water, fields, flowers, mountains, glass, children, parents, organ music or the moon you will marry within a year. If you dream of animals, fishes, birds, giants, paper, a mirror or the sun you will wait five years for your wedding. If you dream of bells, gold, storms, reptiles or soldiers, you will not marry at all.

To find out who will be the first to marry amongst a number of unattached young women, deal around clockwise a pack of ordinary cards and the lass who receives the King of Hearts will be the first to wed. Significant card for men is the Queen of Hearts. Another method depends on having an odd number of people of either sex of up to nine. A pack of well-shuffled cards is placed in a box, and the people make a circle around it. Each person must draw a card in turn around the circle clockwise until there are no more cards left. The drawer of the Ace will be the first to marry, and the possessor of the Ace of Spades will never wed at all.

Cherry Stones

This year, next year, sometime, never, is the incantation with which we count our food stones or strip a daisy bare. To find out who, as well as when, we will wed — Tinker, Tailor, Soldier, Sailor, Rich Man, Poor Man, Beggar-man, Thief, and the lesser known — Army, Navy, Peerage, Trade, Doctor, Divinity, Law.

The Photograph and the Ring

Take a photograph of the one you love and hold a ring tied on a thread of cotton in front of the photograph. Be very careful to keep your hand perfectly still. If the ring moves in a circle, you will wed. If it moves backwards and forwards it is unlikely. If the ring remains stationary you may marry, or not marry at all. (At least not for a long time.)

The Row of Pins

On St Agnes' Eve, i.e. the night before 21 January, take a row of pins out of their paper, put them on a black pin-cushion, one by one, then take them out, sticking a pin in your sleeve as you say a Paternoster. And when you have put them all in your sleeve you will dream of your future husband.

Four Leaf Clover

If you are single and you find one of these, place it in your right shoe and the next new acquaintance who is unattached will be your true love.

The New Moon

Look at the New Moon through a silk handkerchief saying 'New moon

I hail thee. New moon be generous to me. I long to marry. How many moons will it be?' The number of moons seen through the handkerchief will tell you how many months will pass before you marry.

It is said that if you open your bedroom windows, sit on the window-sill on the first night of the New Moon saying, 'All hail Silene, All hail to thee, I prithee good moon reveal to me, This night to whom awedded be,' you will dream of your future husband that night.

Wedding Cake
If you take a small piece of wedding cake, pass it three times through a ring and place it under your pillow, you will dream of your future mate.

Apple Peel
If you peel an apple carefully in one long piece and throw it over your left shoulder with your right hand, to the floor, it will assume the shape of an initial , which will be the first letter of your future husband's first name.

An Old Custom
Girls blindfolded and in pairs would go into a field of cabbages, then holding hands, they would walk until they found a cabbage stalk which they would pull out of the ground. If earth clung to the stalk, their husbands would be wealthy. If the stalk was clean, then the opposite would prevail. Their future husbands would be short, tall, crooked, straight, soft or hard, according to the characteristics of the cabbage.

In Elizabethan days a spell which would reveal a future husband required the swallowing of nine pills made of grated walnut, hazelnut and nutmeg mixed with butter and sugar. The dreams would be of gold, gems, silks, and satins if he were to be rich. Of white linen for a clergyman, darkness for a lawyer, noise and bustle for a tradesman, thunder and lightning for a soldier or sailor, and rain and sleet for a clerk, scribe or a servant.

Wedding Superstitions
June is the favourite marriage month because it was dedicated in Roman times to Juno, wife of Jupiter, protector of women and patroness of marriage. The Romans considered 'May an unlikely marriage month,

but June was good to the man, and happy to the maid.' Sunday was never popular as a wedding day with Christians and Friday, according to Christian tradition, was the day of Our Lord's Crucifixion and also the traditional day upon which Adam ate the forbidden fruit. The Norsemen and Romans both considered Friday lucky; however, there is an old rhyme:

> Monday for health,
> Tuesday for wealth,
> Wednesday the best day of all,
> Thursday for losses,
> Friday for crosses,
> Saturday no luck at all.

But, contrary to this, Saturday seems the most popular day in this era with Wednesday coming a close second. The bridal trousseau used to be cut and sewn by the bride herself, to ensure marital bliss, but the gown was usually made by her friends. If unmarried, they would sew one of their hairs from their own heads into the hem or fold to ensure that their marriages would follow soon. White was chosen as the symbol of purity, simplicity and candour. The Ancient Greek and Roman brides wore yellow veils, which completely covered them during the ceremony. Green is considered unlucky for a bride; blue is the lover's colour and tradition decrees a bride should wear — something old, something new, something borrowed, something blue. Orange blossom is a comparatively recent decoration in England and the U.S.A. It found its way over from France in the early eighteen hundreds, symbolizing purity and fruitfulness, as does the chaplet of flowers, and the bouquet. Corn was worn or carried by the bride of the middle ages.

The Bride on the Wedding Day
The girl is lucky if she wakens to the singing of birds, for it means that she will not have many quarrels throughout her married life. If she finds a spider on her wedding gown, this is a sign that she will have wealth and plenty. A curious custom of the last century was that the bride should feed the cat before she left for the church. If it was

black and rubbed against her, this, too was a fortunate sign. A second one was after her final glance in the mirror before leaving the house, it was traditional that a bride should add either a brooch or a posy, or don her gloves to protect her against bad luck.

She must not cry before her wedding for it augers unhappiness. And should she see a dove, a spider, a black cat, a lamb, or a toad, the marriage will bring her good fortune. However, if she sees a cock or a pig, future discord is predicted. 'Put your right foot forward' must surely have come from this superstition, for it was believed that a bride must enter the church with her right foot first and be sure not to stumble. The young couple must remember to smile at each other at the altar when they meet, as this is considered to bring good luck.

The bridegroom has an easier time — there are not many superstitions appertaining to the bridegroom. The strongest of them all is that it is deemed unlucky for a prospective bridegroom to see his love before the ceremony takes place, and particularly not to see her in bridal array. To make sure of this, he must keep his back turned until she has arrived at his side at the altar. If he has forgotten anything he must not turn back but ask the best man to fetch it.

Rules of the Ring

It is bad luck to drop the ring or to fumble with it. The ring finger was chosen because of the ancient belief that it connects the heart through a nerve from the finger. And the ring must be placed as far down on the finger as possible, as failure to do this is thought to mean an early parting. If the bride has to help him place the ring on her finger, then it is she who will rule the roost after marriage. Symbolizing the never-ending devotion which the man promises to bestow, the ring has an ancient history, and was possibly once used as a talisman of good luck. Documents were sealed with rings in ancient days and rings were given as a symbol of authority which the woman accepted.

The groomsmen are a survival of the days when the marriage was made by capture and the success of the expedition often was made possible by the sturdy band of followers the bridegroom collected around him to help him in the affray, when, with the best man by his side, he snatched the maiden from the bosom of her clan.

After the Wedding

Rice throwing came from the Indian custom connected with wheat ears, which was once an ancient custom in Britain: a symbolic gesture made to ensure abundance and fruitfulness for the happy couple. Confetti was used later, as the hard rice could be injurious to the face and eyes.

Who Will Marry Next?

The bridemaids compete, either for a garter which is thrown, or the bride's bouquet or part of it. The girl who catches the flower or lace will be the next to marry. However, the old saying 'three times a bridesmaid, never a bride' should be remembered, and if a bridesmaid is older than the bride, she must wear something green or she will find she will be left on the shelf.

Reception

The wedding cake dates back to Roman times but the modern counterpart has nothing in common with the simple breadlike mixture of flour, water and salt, that the ancients ate in the belief that it would shield them from want and poverty. Icing and ornaments were introduced about the time of the Stuarts, and today it is an elaborate structure which dominates the wedding feast. To drink the bride's health in anything but alcohol bodes ill for the bride, and to refuse to eat a little portion of the cake means that you are thinking ill of the bride.

Throwing a Shoe

As the bride goes up the stairs to prepare for the honeymon journey, it was an old tradition, a little like the throwing of the bouquet, that she threw one shoe over her left shoulder, and whoever caught it, male or female would, if unmarried, be the next to marry.

Unlucky Pins

Any pins used in the wedding attire must either be thrown away or given to the attendants, but never used again, as this will bring bad luck, and the honeymoon will be unhappy.

The Symbolic Shoe

The custom of attaching a shoe to the vehicle in which the young married couple drive away, or throwing a shoe at them, is very ancient. It dates either from the Anglo-Saxon custom of the father of the bride giving the groom one of the bride's shoes, with which he touched her gently on the head as a reminder of his authority over her; or from the time when brides were carried off by force, and this symbol of violence survived.

Honeymoon

The Teutons celebrated a wedding for thirty days after the event, by drinking mead, which is made from honey, and the bride and bridegroom took part in this marathon event. Occasional quarrels on the honeymoon are seen as a sign of future harmony, but both bride and groom must be careful not to break anything whilst honeymooning, especially a mirror. The bride should wear green frequently on her honeymoon for it is supposed to bring much love.

The Home-Coming

The custom that a bride should be carried over the threshold originated in Scotland, but with the added ritual of her mother-in-law breaking shortbread over her head to ensure plenty. In Ireland an oaten cake is broken over the bride's head to ensure against want. An old English custom was to pour boiling water on the threshold before the bride enters, whilst in some countries it was considered lucky if the newly-wed bride placed dough on the floor of her house to indicate that she in future would be housekeeper there.

Rings

Never put on a wedding ring before the wedding. To lose a ring, either a wedding or engagement ring, foretells a future break.

The Language of Rings

A ring on the first finger of the left hand means 'I wish to marry'. A ring on the third finger of the left hand means 'I am engaged or married'. A ring on the second finger of the left hand means 'I prefer platonic friendship'. And a ring on the little finger of the left hand means 'I never intend to marry'. An offer of marriage should be made on a Friday evening to ensure good fortune and the announcement of an engagement on a Saturday to bring good luck. Lovers should avoid meeting each other on the stairs and kissing there, for this brings bad luck.

Love letters should only be written in blue ink or pencil. Three kisses is the luckiest number to append at the close of a love-letter, but *never* should they number four, seven or thirteen. Never post a letter on Christmas Day or 29 February in Leap Year. Take care not to drop a love-letter when going to post it: next time you meet your lover you will surely quarrel. It is lucky to finish a love-letter as the clock strikes midnight, and to post it under a full moon.

Chapter 13

Old Superstitions and Ancient Omens

To kiss for the first time under a new moon brings exceptional good fortune, a marriage which will be happy and well endowed. If a girl in love falls upstairs, this is believed to portend an early marriage. Lovers should avoid meeting by poplar trees for they spell inconstancy, they should meet either on a hillside, on the seashore, by a river or deep in a grove of trees, for it is said that then neither will be untrue or inconstant. Neither crossroads nor bridges should ever be used as trysting-places. If you meet either a white horse or black cat, when walking with your lover, it is believed that it will be a wonderful marriage. Blue is the colour for lovers — turquoise the Lucky Stone. It's an old superstition that a lock of the loved one's hair tied in a lover's knot, or half a sixpence, kept by each of the lovers, would ensure constancy. Sweethearts should not look together through glass at the new moon for it will bring bad luck.

Cock Crowing
For a girl to hear a cock crowing while thinking of her lover is a good sign. But to hear a cock crowing on your wedding day portends strife and quarrels throughout your married life.

Dove
A sign of bliss and contentment in love.

Pigeon
A white pigeon flying around a dwelling means an engagement or the imminent marriage of one of the inmates of the dwelling.

Sparrow
A fortunate bird for lovers.

Lamb
To meet a solitary lamb presages love, peace and prosperity.

Mouse
To be presented with a white mouse by one who is unaware of the significance of his gift will bring happiness in love.

Pig
An unlucky sign if seen by a wedding party, for it means an unhappy marriage.

Squirrel
To see a squirrel means happiness is near.

Rose
An unexpected gift of roses is lucky for the lover.

Wistaria
To come upon a hidden wistaria in bloom means you will receive a communication from someone who loves you but you have not seen for a long time.

Fateful Year
The thirty-first year for a woman is supposed to be a fateful year in her life and changes usually occur at this time. The change usually has something to do with an important journey, unexpected danger or great temptation. It is a period which requires great caution.

Hand
To knock your hand against a piece of wood or wooden article accidentally means a love affair is imminent. To knock your hand against iron is a warning against false friends and heartbreaks.

Knife
Crossed knives mean bad luck and quarrels. To drop a knife means a visit from a male friend. A present of a knife must always be paid for with small coins so that the friendship will not be cut.

Matches
If a girl accidentally spills a box of matches she will soon become a bride. Two matches crossed by accident means joy and happiness in the near future. Carry a nutmeg in your handbag and you will be sure of marriage to an elderly suitor. Never give the man you are going to marry slippers, or knit a sweater for him or weave any clothing for him; never be photographed and never sit on a table while talking to him, or you will never marry him.

Hallowe'en: Bobbing for Apples
Each person is given an apple from which a small piece has been cut to allow a fortune, written on a small slip of paper, to be inserted. The apples are thrown in a large tub of water and the people are invited to duck their heads, and retrieve an apple in their mouth — keeping their arms behind their backs. They then read aloud their fortunes, which, of necessity, are brief, such as 'beware of the dark man who professes to be your friend', or 'you will marry a man of great learning'.

Hallowe'en Lucky Dip
Mashed potato is the traditional dish and six charms are placed in it. Then all the lights are extinguished and the guests with spoon and fork try to find the hidden charms, which are:

> A ring — marriage
> A coin — wealth
> A button — bachelorhood
> A heart shaped charm — passionate love
> A shell — long journeys
> A key — great success and power

To See Your Future Husband at Hallowe'en
Retire with one lighted candle into a darkened room. Sit before a mirror

either eating an apple or combing your hair. After a few minutes it is said that you will see the face of your future husband looking over your shoulder.

Christmas Spells
Here are a few Christmas spells which are easy and very ancient.

Leaves of Holly
Take three leaves of holly, and prick with a pin the initials of your admirers, place them under your pillow and go to sleep. The one of whom you dream will be your future husband. Tie a sprig of holly to each leg of your bed, and before you retire to bed, eat a baked or roasted apple. Your future husband will be revealed to you in your dreams.

New Year's Eve
Drink the last glass from a bottle, before the clock has finished striking twelve, and you will be the first girl of the house or party to marry.

New Year's Day
Should a young girl arise and look out of her window and see a man passing by, she will be married within the year.

The Witches' Sabbath
You will need a large black velvet pin-cushion, and the smallest pins, you can find. With these you make your name on one side, and on the other with very large pins, you make a cross within a circle. Then you place the pin-cushion in your left stocking, and hang it at the foot of your bed. You will dream of your future life with the man you will marry. If early on the Midsummer's Eve morning after fasting, you go into a garden and gather St John's wort, whilst fresh with dew, you will marry within the year.

St Valentine's Day
The year will be a single one if the first person you meet after leaving the house on the morning of 14 February is a person of the same sex. If a woman, and you meet a man, then you will meet your fate within

three months, and if he is unmarried, he could be your future husband. If you have no valentines, take two bay leaves sprinkled with rosewater and lay them on your pillow when you go to bed. Don clean night attire making sure that it is put on *inside-out* then say 'in dreams good valentine be kind to me and let me this one night my true love see'.

May Day
'The girl who on the first of May, goes to the fields at break of day, and washes in dew from the hawthorn tree, ever more beautiful shall she be.' At dawn on 1 May search for a garden snail, and place it by the ashes of a dead fire. If the snail draws in its horns and refuses to move, there will be no romance for you. If it crawls away it will leave a trail in the shape of an initial, which will indicate your future lover.

Lent
Marry in the Lent, sure to repent.

CHAPTER 14

Talismans to Protect Your Love

Charms and Talismans

Talisman comes from the Arabic word 'Tilsam' and the later Greek 'Telesma', meaning mystery. A Talisman is an object which is believed to avert danger and bring fortune and there are many which have come to use from antiquity such as the Seal of Solomon, the Cross, the Swastika, the Hand of Fatima, the Fish, and the Horn of Plenty. These mascots, fortified by the faith of the wearer, become an ever-present force by constant possession. Displaying the lucky object may have no occult power whatsoever, but simply bring a desired result through auto-suggestion, and through the third power of the believer. However, from time immemorial, there have been a few of these Telesma dedicated to lovers, and it is with these we are concerned.

Beads
Amber beads are lucky for brides.

Eye Beads
'Those shaped as an eye, in blue glass or onyx, are said to promote love affairs.'

Fish
An emblem of fish was an ancient Egyptian charm for domestic happiness.

Frog
The ancient Romans considered this the lover's talisman ensuring happy

relationships and promoting mutual ardour.

Heart
The symbol of love universal and considered to be the seat of the soul. This is worn to bring constancy and joy.

The Horseshoe
Worn as a crescent on the shoes of Roman matrons, it was considered to ward off moon madness and hysteria, and ensure happy motherhood.

Keys
A Japanese charm depicting the keys of a granary, and a popular talisman for wealth, love and general happiness.

The Talisman of Venus

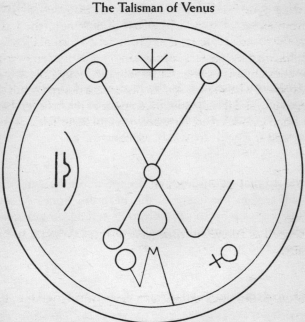

The Talisman of Venus
The seal of the goddess also known as Aphrodite, the ruler of love and beauty, was a very powerful talisman. It should be drawn on

parchment or thick paper and carried on the person, particularly when travelling.

The Magic Property of Precious Stones

Magical and astrological significance has been given to precious stones, since the earliest of the world's civilizations. Amulets and talismans containing gems were fashioned, many to protect the wearer from the evil eyes and to bring protection and relief from illness, but some were worn to attract love and to bring good fortune to the lover. We are going to list a few of these.

Aquamarine

Its name was taken from the Latin words meaning sea-water or blue-green, because of its beautiful colour which was thought by the Romans to resemble the sea and to be both a lucky keystone for seafarers, and a jewel that brought harmony into a marriage.

Diamond

In Roman days this gem was often bound to a warrior's left arm to imbue him with courage. It is the lover's stone, worn to promote constancy and fortitude through the trials of married life, and was thought to be a token of reconciliation and a measure towards in attainment.

Emerald

It was believed that inconstancy or deception on the part of a lover was enough to dim the lustre of this beautiful stone. An outright treachery could cause it to crumble in its setting. An ancient belief connected with the emerald is that it wards off dangers, and lessens the pains of childbirth.

Garnet

The emblem of constancy and faithfulness between friends and lovers.

Jet

A compact form of coal, this stone was considered to have curative properties for the female. Ancient authorities stated that the fumes of this mineral when burnt would indicate whether a woman was chaste or not, and it was worn as a protection against hysteria and female disorders, and also as a counter-agent to magical spells and occult influences.

Sapphire
An age-old stone mentioned in the scriptures, this beautiful variety of Corundum was thought to promote mental health and if worn over the heart, was thought to strengthen that organ. It was said to guard the chastity of the wearer and would dim in warning at the approach of treachery or evil.

Sardonyx
This stone, like the emerald, was thought to lessen the pains of childbirth. Brides in ancient Rome wore this stone to bring marital happiness.

Turquoise
Found mainly in Persia, this stone is considered to be the luckiest stone for lovers. It gives protection against the evil intentions of others. It was also once worn by horsemen to ensure sure-footedness, and was supposed to promote peace and harmony in marriage.

Ancient Word Talismans

Abracadabra is said to be derived from the Hebrew words 'Ha, Brachab Dababarah' which means 'Speak the blessings'. It was used as a charm or amulet for protection against disease. Indeed, Daniel Defoe tells of the panic-stricken inhabitants of plague-ridden London hanging these same amulets around their necks on a piece of silk, in 1665. It was written in this way, to make a triangle, which was considered to be the occult symbol of perfection.

```
A B R A C A D A B R A
A B R A C A D A B R
A B R A C A D A B
A B R A C A D A
A B R A C A D
A B R A C A
A B R A C
A B R A
A B R
A B
A
```

Groups of words, reading forwards, downwards, backwards and upwards were popular as amulets against accidents and evil spirits. Sometimes they were found on the walls of dwelling or temples, more often they were worn for personal protection, such as the following example which was once widely used.

```
S A T O R
A R E P O
T E N E T
O P E R A
R O T A S
```

The true significance has been lost but the literal translation of these words is as follows:

> Sator means the Sower,
> Arepo means the Plough,
> Tenet means holds,
> Opera means tasks or works,
> Rotas means wheels.

The Pentacle, or the five pointed star, which is a form of the Seal of Solomon, has long been regarded as having great occult powers. It is symbolized as a way to high endeavours and great achievement and also as a protector of bodily health.

The Tetragrammaton

This is a mystic name used by the Ancient Jews. It consisted of a piece of parchment inscribed with certain symbols enclosed in a calfskin bag and worn either on the left arm or on the forehead. Sometimes the names of the angels, Michael, Gabriel and Raphael were included in a Tetragrammaton which also enclosed a five pointed star within a circle or series of circles inside which the word Tetragrammaton was split into five syllables and distributed within each point of the star.

The Seven Angel Talisman

One of the oldest and considered by the ancients to be the most powerful of all talismans is the Seven Angel Talisman. This consists of a large circle containing the double interlacing triangle or the Jewish 'Shield of David' as it is known. The Latin motto 'Via invia virtuti nulla est' — there is no way impassable to virtue — is placed within the small triangles at the tips of five of the points while the word and symbol

The Talisman
of the Angels

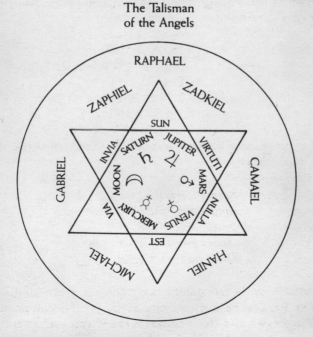

for sun is placed in the topmost point. The names of the planets are placed around the inner triangle. Their order is Saturn, Jupiter at the top, Mars at the right side, Venus at the bottom, and Mercury Moon on the left side. Raphael is placed above the sun and under it either side are the names Zaphiel and Zadkiel, and running clockwise around the outer circle to follow these two are Camael, Haniel, Michael and Gabriel, so that the angels are directly above the planets they govern. Zaphiel governs Saturn, Zadkiel governs Jupiter, Camael governs Mars, Raphael governs the Sun, Haniel governs Venus, Michael governs Mercury, Gabriel governs the Moon.

Index